BRONTË PARSONAGE MUSEUM, HAWORTH

A Souvenir Guide

Ann Dinsdale, Librarian
& Kathryn White, Curator

Photographs by Simon Warner

The Brontë Society
1998

Brontë

FAMILY TREE

Hugh Brunty
born 1755
died c. 1808

married 1776

Eleanor McClory (Alice)

Thomas Branwell
born 1746
died 5.4.1808

married 1768

Anne Carne
baptised 27.4.1744
died 19.12.1809

Patrick Brontë (Brunty)
born 17.3.1777
died 7.6.1861

married 29.12.1812

Maria Branwell
born 15.4.1783
died 15.9.1821

Elizabeth Branwell (Aunt Branwell)
born 1776
died 29.10.1842

Maria
born 1814
died 6.5.1825

Elizabeth
born 8.2.1815
died 15.6.1825

Patrick Branwell
born 26.6.1817
died 24.9.1848

Emily Jane
born 30.7.1818
died 19.12.1848

Anne
born 17.1.1820
died 28.5.1849

Arthur Bell Nicholls
born 1818
died 3.12.1906

married 29.6.1854

Charlotte
born 21.4.1816
died 31.3.1855

CONTENTS

INTRODUCTION

Who were the Brontës?

The Brontës were the world's most famous literary family and Haworth Parsonage, now the Brontë Parsonage Museum, was their home from 1820 to 1861. Charlotte, Emily and Anne Brontë were the authors of some of the best-loved books in the English language. Charlotte's novel *Jane Eyre* (1847), Emily's *Wuthering Heights* (1847) and Anne's *The Tenant of Wildfell Hall* (1848) were written in this house over a hundred and fifty years ago, yet their power still moves readers today. To find two writers of genius in one family would be rare, but to find several writers in one household is unique in the history of literature. Charlotte and Emily are ranked among the world's greatest novelists; Anne is a powerful but underrated author, and both their father, the Revd. Patrick Brontë, and brother Branwell also saw their own works in print. The Brontës' novels, published under the pseudonyms of Currer, Ellis and Acton Bell, were acknowledged at the time for their directness and powerful emotional energy, qualities which were sometimes interpreted by the critics as 'coarse' and 'brutal'.

Myth and Reality

Surprisingly, the enduring myth of the Brontës living a life of unrelieved isolation and tragedy was, to some extent, created unintentionally by the Brontës themselves. In choosing to write under pseudonyms, the sisters drew an immediate veil of mystery around them, and people speculated as to the true identity of Currer, Ellis and Acton Bell. After Emily's and Anne's early deaths, Charlotte added to the legend in her 1850 *Biographical Notice* of her sisters. To protect Emily and Anne from the accusations of brutality levelled by the critics, Charlotte portrayed her sisters as unlearned, unworldly young women who wrote by instinct rather than design.

The novelist Elizabeth Gaskell was Charlotte's first biographer and she was responsible for perpetuating a wider knowledge of the Brontës' lives when she published *The Life of Charlotte Brontë* in 1857, two years after Charlotte's death. Gaskell's book, which stands today as one of the best biographical

Above: Title pages of first editions of the Brontës' novels.
Left: Branwell Brontë's famous portrait of Anne, Emily and Charlotte Brontë was painted around 1834, when Branwell was seventeen, and the original painting is now in the National Portrait Gallery. The gap between Emily and Charlotte is where Branwell painted out a portrait of himself, probably because the composition was unbalanced. The creases on the canvas show where Charlotte's widower, Arthur Bell Nicholls, folded the painting for storage.

studies of its kind, was nevertheless approached from a novelist's perspective and it became a monument to what she perceived as Charlotte's tragedy of noble self-sacrifice to duty. Thus the Brontës were elevated to the mythic, heroic status which is so often applied to those who die young. The Brontë Parsonage Museum seeks to separate myth from reality and to present the known facts about the family.

The Influence of their Home Environment

Charlotte, Branwell, Emily and Anne were born at Thornton, near Bradford, but moved to the nearby township of Haworth when Charlotte, the eldest of the famous novelists, was barely five years old. The children's formative years and their mature writing careers were developed in Haworth, amid the dramatic landscape of the surrounding moors. Early biographers and critics sometimes assumed that the Brontës based their fiction exclusively on real life places, people and events, perhaps unwilling to accept that the daughters of a clergyman could produce what were often perceived as shocking, amoral books. However, this would be to deny the Brontës the power of imagination. The Parsonage was the home in which the young Brontës' creativity was nurtured, where they created their childhood lands of Angria and Gondal, and in which they served a collaborative literary apprenticeship of over twenty years prior to the publication of their novels. Like most authors, the Brontës drew upon their imaginations, on their personal experiences and the landscape and characters around them, but their mature poems and novels are also rooted in the themes of the early writings of their childhood and adolescence.

The Brontës and Victorian Society

The Brontës occupied an unusual position in society, one which was to influence the themes of their novels. The Parsonage was amongst the largest houses in Haworth, though in comparison with the homes of clergymen in more affluent areas of Britain, it would have been considered small. Similarly, Patrick's annual income of around £200 was twenty times more than that of the average domestic servant, but the Brontës were poor in comparison with landowners or wealthy aristocrats whose income might exceed £10,000 or even £20,000. In the early nineteenth century, the class system was a much more rigid structure than today. The Brontës' education, in the era prior to the 1870 Elementary Education Act, when a large proportion of the population could not read, placed them socially above most people in Haworth. However, the Brontës could not afford to keep a carriage, to travel extensively, or to dress and furnish their home as did the upper classes and wealthy manufacturers of Yorkshire. It was essential that the Brontë girls earned a living, and their experience as governesses, a social hinterland where they were neither family nor servant, informed much of their writing.

Visiting the home in which these three remarkable women spent most of their lives provides a fascinating insight into the freedoms and restrictions of the time in which they lived and thus a deeper understanding of their novels.

Above: The Haworth Moors, a constant source of delight for all the Brontë children, by E.M. Wimperis, from the first illustrated edition of Wuthering Heights, *Smith Elder & Co., 1872.*

THE MOORS

'Wuthering Heights is the name of Mr Heathcliff's dwelling, "Wuthering" being a significant provincial adjective, descriptive of the atmospheric tumult to which its station is exposed in stormy weather. Pure, bracing ventilation they must have up there, at all times, indeed: one may guess the power of the north wind, blowing over the edge, by the excessive slant of a few, stunted firs at the end of the house; and by a range of gaunt thorns all stretching their limbs one way, as if craving alms of the sun.' Emily Brontë, *Wuthering Heights* (1847).

Although Haworth itself was a dour industrial township in the Brontës' day, the landscape which most people associate with the family is the haunting, windswept moorland which extends for mile after mile beyond their parsonage home. When the Brontës were alive, the moors were less isolated: the now disused Penistone quarries offered employment to large numbers of men, and the farmhouses, now

Below: Top Withens farm lies about four miles from Haworth Parsonage. It has often been associated with Wuthering Heights, *and though it is possible that Emily Brontë had the moorland setting of Withens in mind when she wrote her novel, the old, now-ruined farmhouse bears no similarity to the house she described.*

ruined, were inhabited by the hardy few who eked out a living from subsistence farming.

Life was harsh for the moorland farmers, and in *The Life of Charlotte Brontë* Elizabeth Gaskell described how 'the snow lay long and late on the moors…' She noted how only the hardiest flowers would grow in the Parsonage garden, and how 'on autumnal or winter nights, the four winds of heaven seemed to meet and rage together, tearing round the house as if they were wild beasts striving to find an entrance.' The weather is a force to be reckoned with in Haworth, and in the Brontë novels it is used with great effect to heighten human states of being and emotion. The majority of Charlotte's surviving letters contain references to the weather, and for those with constitutions already weakened by constant exposure to disease and infection, the change of seasons could be a matter of life or death. Shortly after Emily's funeral, Charlotte wrote: 'no need now to tremble for the hard frost and keen wind - Emily does not feel them.'

After the deaths of her sisters, Charlotte wrote of the moorland around Haworth: '…when I go out there alone everything reminds me of the times when others were with me, and then the moors seem a wilderness, featureless, solitary, saddening. My sister Emily had a particular love for them, and there is not a knoll of heather, not a branch of fern, not a young bilberry leaf, not a fluttering lark or linnet, but reminds me of her. The distant prospects were Anne's delight, and when I look round she is in the blue tints, the pale mists, the waves and shadows of the horizon. In the hill-country silence their poetry comes by lines and stanzas into my mind: once I loved it; now I dare not read it…'

LIFE AND DEATH IN HAWORTH

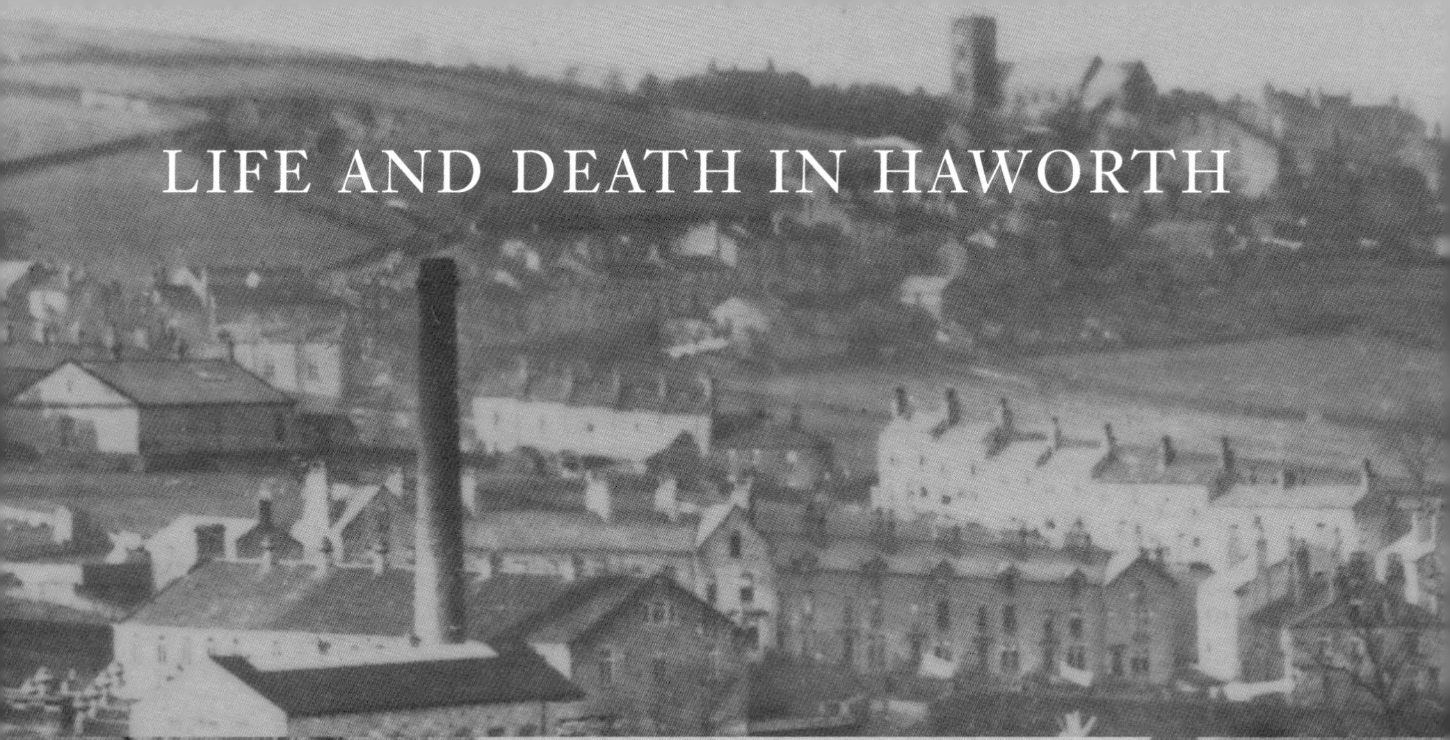

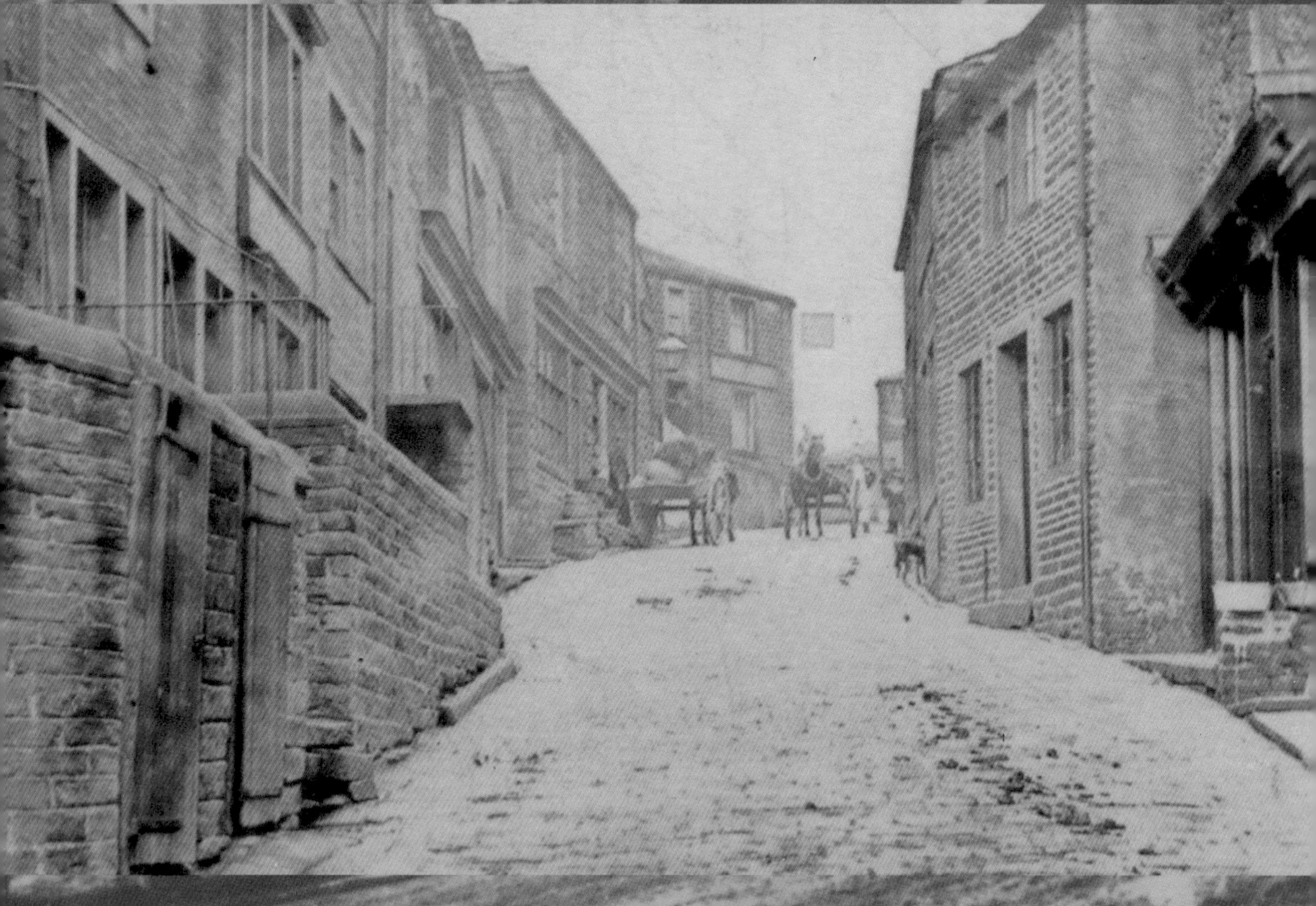

D espite its lofty hill-top setting and the openness of the surrounding moorland, Haworth township was an overcrowded and unhealthy place in which to live in the Brontës' day. A report compiled by Benjamin Babbage for the General Board of Health, published in 1850, attributed much of this ill health to the cramped conditions in which the inhabitants lived and worked, the lack of privies (only 1 to every 4.5 houses), and the fact that the only sewerage system consisted of open channels running down the Main Street. It therefore comes as no surprise to learn from Elizabeth Gaskell's 1857 biography of Charlotte that the Brontës took their walks, 'rather out towards the heathery moors…than towards the long descending village street.'

All these hazards to public health were exacerbated by the poor water supply, which was not only inadequate for the needs of the population, but contaminated by deadly seepage from the graveyard above the village, the privies, and the overflowing midden heaps which littered the streets. In some ways the Brontës fared better than their neighbours: the Parsonage had its own two-seater privy and a private well fed by the moorland springs. However, their close proximity to the ill-drained, dangerously over-filled graveyard was a constant threat to their health. When Babbage conducted his investigation, he noted that there had been 1,344 burials in the previous ten years alone, and he recommended that the graveyard be closed immediately. He was also alarmed by the Haworth practice of covering graves with large flat stones which prevented the growth of plants which would assist decomposition.

Above: Haworth Old Church and churchyard c. 1860. With the exception of the tower, the church was demolished in 1879 and rebuilt on the same site.

Right: The Black Bull, Haworth, c. 1856. In 1850 Haworth was served by seven public houses and three beer shops. Although alcoholism contributed to Branwell Brontë's death, consumption of beer and spirits in Haworth is said to have been below average.

Although tragic, the Brontë deaths were unremarkable in a village where forty-one per cent of children died before reaching the age of six. The Babbage report concluded that the average life expectancy of twenty-five years corresponded with that of some of the most unhealthy districts of London. Health improvements to Haworth, for which Patrick Brontë himself had campaigned, came too late to benefit his own family, and the many gravestones commemorating the deaths of young children stand as sad reminders of the suffering which was commonplace in the Brontës' day.

Left: Haworth Old Church and Parsonage, photographed before 1878. Right: Elizabeth Gaskell's drawing of the same scene. Below: A modern view of Haworth Church and Parsonage.

HAWORTH PARSONAGE

Haworth Parsonage, built in 1778-9, became the home of the Brontë family in 1820, when Mr Brontë was appointed perpetual curate of the Church. The Parsonage came rent-free with Patrick's new position, and was to be the family's home for the rest of their lives. The fact that Mr Brontë had no independent means was a source of anxiety for the family, for if his health failed, they stood to lose both income and home. In the event, Patrick outlived all his family.

After Patrick Brontë's death in 1861, Haworth Parsonage became the home of his successor, the Revd. John Wade. Wade evidently found the Parsonage cramped and inconvenient, and in 1878 outraged many Brontë enthusiasts when he added a large gabled wing to create more space for his growing family. Other internal alterations were made to the Brontë part of the house, including the addition of new fireplaces and the removal of the old kitchen range. The Brontës' kitchen became a virtual passageway to Wade's new extension.

Above: The Parsonage showing the large gabled wing which was added in 1878 by Revd. Wade. The barn, which was used as a stonemason's workshop in the Brontës' time, was demolished in 1903.

Above: The Revd. John Wade, Incumbent of Haworth 1861-1898. Left: A view of the Parsonage showing the rear of the building before the addition of the 1960s extension.

Before its acquisition by the Brontë Society, the Parsonage served as home to three more incumbents: T.W. Story (1898-1919); G.A. Elson (1919-1925) and J.C. Hirst (1925-1928). In 1928, Sir James Roberts, a local man who had made a fortune in the textile industry, bought the Parsonage for the Society and provided the money to set it up as a museum. In the Museum's early days the Wade wing was adapted to serve as a Research Library and living accommodation for the resident Custodian. Over the years further extensions to the rear of the building have created more exhibition space.

Despite the addition of the Wade wing, and the trees which now soften the bleak graveyard prospect, the original Georgian Parsonage is still very much as the Brontës would have known it.

The majority of the rooms in the original Brontë part of the house are set out in as close an approximation as possible to their appearance in the Brontës' day, and most of the objects and furniture on display actually belonged to the family. For conservation reasons, the exhibits are changed regularly and you may not always see exactly what is described in this souvenir guide.

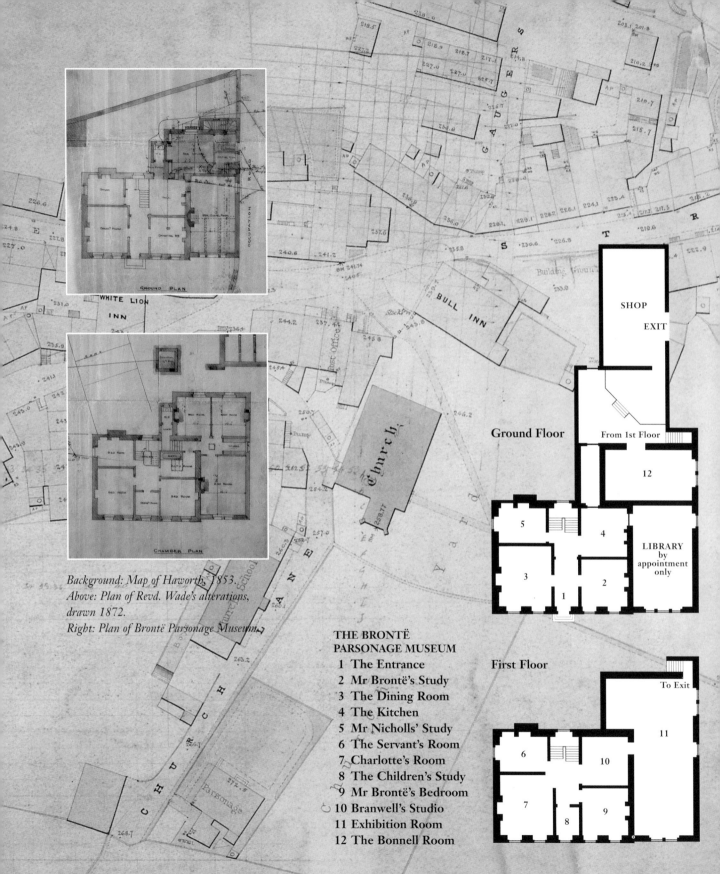

Background: Map of Haworth, 1853.
Above: Plan of Revd. Wade's alterations, drawn 1872.
Right: Plan of Brontë Parsonage Museum.

THE BRONTË PARSONAGE MUSEUM

1 The Entrance
2 Mr Brontë's Study
3 The Dining Room
4 The Kitchen
5 Mr Nicholls' Study
6 The Servant's Room
7 Charlotte's Room
8 The Children's Study
9 Mr Brontë's Bedroom
10 Branwell's Studio
11 Exhibition Room
12 The Bonnell Room

Ground Floor

SHOP
EXIT
From 1st Floor
12
LIBRARY by appointment only
5
4
3
2
1

First Floor

To Exit
11
6
10
7
8
9

THE ENTRANCE HALL

In her 1871 *Reminiscences*, Charlotte's close schoolfriend Ellen Nussey recalled her first visit to the Parsonage in the summer of 1833, and how, after family prayers at eight o'clock, Mr Brontë would lock and bar the front door at nine, '…always giving as he passed the sitting-room door a kindly admonition to the "children" not to be late; half-way up the stairs he stayed his steps to wind up the clock…' She added, 'The hall floor and stairs were done with sand-stone, always beautifully clean, as was everything about the house', and described the walls as being, 'not papered, but stained in a pretty dove-coloured tint'. The entrance hall would have been larger than it is today, as Charlotte widened the dining room at the expense of the hall when she had several structural alterations made to the building in 1850.

In a letter to a friend, Elizabeth Gaskell said: 'I don't know that I ever saw a spot more exquisitely clean…Everything fits into, and is in harmony with, the idea of a country parsonage, possessed by people of very moderate means.' The furnishings in the Parsonage reflect the simplicity of the late Georgian and early Victorian period. Ellen described the effect as 'scant and bare indeed' but nevertheless, 'mind and thought, I had almost said elegance but certainly refinement, diffused themselves over all, and made nothing really wanting.' Although Ellen stated that 'there was not much carpet anywhere', except in the dining room and Mr Brontë's study, a stair carpet and stair rods were sold at the 1861 sale, along with several other 'Kiddiminster Carpets and Rugs'. Ellen also recalled that Mr Brontë was fearful that the combination of young children, candles and curtains would be a fire hazard. The windows were shuttered at

This mahogany long case clock, made by Barraclough of Haworth, stood halfway up the stairs. Mr Brontë wound it every night at nine o'clock.

night and curtains were introduced at a later date. An early ambrotype photograph of the Parsonage shows a combination of shutters, blinds and curtains in use in the 1850s. Charlotte purchased curtains for the dining room in 1851 and for her husband's study prior to their marriage in 1854. Damask and muslin curtains are also recorded in the 1861 Bill of Sale. Wallpaper and curtains throughout the house are based on designs of the period.

MR BRONTË'S STUDY

The Revd. Patrick Brontë carried out most of his parish business from this room, which he used as his study. In old age, he was described as 'sitting in a plain, uncushioned chair, upright as a soldier' before the fire. Elizabeth Gaskell did not know the young, enthusiastic Patrick Brontë, whose wife Maria addressed him as 'My Dear Saucy Pat' during their courtship. Gaskell did not encounter Mr Brontë until a visit to see her new friend Charlotte in 1853. By then he was unwell, in his seventies and had suffered the

Left: Section from Charlotte's letter to Ellen dated September 1846, in which she discusses Mr Brontë's progress after his recent cataract operation.

Left: Mr Brontë's chair in front of the fireplace.
Below: Mr Brontë's letter of 8 August 1831, concerning the building of the Sunday School, is signed by the church trustees as well as by Mr Brontë.

loss of all but one of his family. Thus Gaskell's sometimes unfavourable presentation of Mr Brontë lacked the dimension of the father whose lively ideas, discussions and encouragement stimulated and informed the minds of his children.

Mr Brontë was a remarkable clergyman, deeply concerned about the welfare of his parishioners, founding a Sunday School and campaigning for improvements in sanitation in Haworth. He was keenly aware of wider religious and political issues and wrote many letters to the newspapers. Mr Brontë was a Church of England clergyman. He did not support the strict Calvinist doctrine of only the 'elect' reaching Heaven and, like his daughter Anne in her novel *The Tenant of Wildfell Hall*, his attitude tended towards the more generous message of forgiveness and hope.

Mr Brontë's eyesight deteriorated with age until he was almost blind. When he was sixty-nine he travelled to a surgeon in Manchester and underwent a cataract operation without anaesthetic which improved his sight, though he continued to wear spectacles and to use a magnifying glass to help him to read. It was while Charlotte was nursing her father in their lodgings in Manchester that she began to write *Jane Eyre*.

It was in this room that Patrick Brontë first discovered that his eldest daughter was a successful author. In a letter of August 1850, Elizabeth Gaskell recounts how when Charlotte, carrying a copy of *Jane Eyre* and some reviews, marched into her father's study, the following exchange took place:

'"Papa, I've been writing a book." "Have you my dear?" and he went on reading. "But Papa, I want you to look at it." "I can't be troubled to read MS." "But it is printed." "I hope you have not been involving yourself in any such silly expense." "I think I shall gain some money by it. May I read you some reviews?"'

Later that day, he announced: '"Children, Charlotte has been writing a book - and I think it is a better one than I expected."' Mr Brontë was always very proud of his children's achievements, attributing their ability in part to his own eccentricity.

Above: Mr Brontë suffered from a delicate stomach and ate many of his meals quietly alone in this room to aid his digestion.
Left: Mr Brontë was photographed several times late in his life.

Mr Brontë, who had fought his way from a humble background in Ireland to Cambridge University, knew the value of education and fostered his children's interest in art, literature, politics and music. Three popular engravings of biblical scenes by John Martin (1789-1854) hung in this room ('The Deluge', 'Belshazzar's Feast' and 'Joshua Commanding the Sun'). Martin's dramatic, large scale pictures were an early inspiration for the young Brontës.

Mr Brontë purchased this 'cabinet' piano for his children. Its strings are arranged vertically, so that the instrument takes up less space. Ellen Nussey described Emily as playing with, 'precision and brilliancy'. She had advanced music lessons from a professor in Brussels and also taught three young pupils there. 'Anne played also', recalled Ellen, 'but she preferred soft harmonies and vocal music. She sang a little; her voice was weak, but very sweet in tone.' Charlotte, it seems, did not play, probably due to her extreme short sight. Anne and Branwell each copied their favourite pieces into manuscript music books. Branwell was an enthusiastic musician, playing the flute and the organ at Haworth Church.

THE DINING ROOM

Charlotte, Emily and Anne did most of their writing here and the room was the focus of their creativity. *Jane Eyre*, *Wuthering Heights* and *Agnes Grey* were written in this room. It was the sisters' habit to walk around the table until about eleven o'clock, reading and discussing their writing plans and projects. After the deaths of Emily and Anne, Charlotte walked in solitude, unable to sleep without this nightly ritual. Martha Brown, servant at the Parsonage, described how, 'My heart aches to hear Miss Brontë walking, walking on alone.'

The dining room would also have been used to entertain visitors, and therefore it is the room most often described in articles and contemporary accounts. Like the bedroom directly above, this room was enlarged by Charlotte in 1850. The dining room, sometimes called the parlour, is furnished in a simple style. Elizabeth Gaskell said, 'The parlour has evidently been refurbished within the last few years, since Miss Brontë's success has enabled her to have a little more money to spend…The prevailing colour of the room is crimson…There is her likeness by Richmond, an engraving from Lawrence's picture of Thackeray, and two recesses, on each side of the high, narrow, old-fashioned mantel-piece, filled with books.' The books on the shelves are of the period, while those owned by the Brontës themselves are stored securely elsewhere. The house would have been lit with a combination of oil lamps, rushlights and candles. Charlotte recalled little about her mother, who died in 1821 when Charlotte was just five years old, but a treasured, vague memory was of Mrs Brontë nursing Branwell in this room.

Above: Copy of George Richmond's portrait of Charlotte Brontë. At her publisher's request Charlotte sat for her portrait to George Richmond (1809-1896) on a visit to London in 1850. The original is now in the National Portrait Gallery. It was used as the basis for the frontispiece to the first edition of Elizabeth Gaskell's 1857 biography of Charlotte.

Above: Emily's diary paper of 26 June 1837 includes this sketch of herself and Anne writing at the table, with the tin box in which they kept the diary papers beside them.
Below: This gate-leg table, in a private collection, is believed to be the original dining room table, sold at the 1861 sale and pictured in the sketch. The pedestal table usually on display in this room was also sold at the 1861 sale, but dates from the later part of the family's time at the Parsonage. It was made by William Wood, the Haworth joiner, who made other furniture for the Brontës.

20

THE DINING ROOM

Top right: Branwell Brontë. A plaster medallion portrait by his friend, Joseph Bentley Leyland (1811-1851), a professional sculptor based in Halifax.

Middle right: William Makepeace Thackeray (1811-1863). An engraving from the 1852 portrait by Samuel Lawrence (1812-1884). Thackeray, the author of Vanity Fair *(1847), was an author greatly admired by Charlotte. This portrait was a present to Charlotte from her publisher.*

Lower right: Arthur Wellesley, Duke of Wellington (1769-1852). An engraving from an 1844 daguerrotype photograph. The Duke of Wellington was a great hero of the Brontë family, and this picture was a present to Mr Brontë from Charlotte's publisher.

Right: Black horsehair sofa made by William Wood for the Brontë family. Emily is reputed to have died in this room at two o'clock in the afternoon of 19 December 1848, refusing to see a doctor until it was too late. The story dates from the 1883 biography of Emily by Mary Robinson, who had interviewed Ellen Nussey and others who knew the Brontës. Robinson describes how Emily's sisters begged to be allowed to put her to bed, and later that day how, 'leaning with one hand upon the sofa', Emily tried to rise and then died. It has been suggested that it is more likely that Emily died upstairs in bed. However, Emily died in winter and the children's study, usually associated with Emily, had no fireplace. She may have slept in a more comfortable room in her last illness, but it is impossible to be certain without further evidence. Ellen recalled that Anne Brontë died on a sofa at their lodgings in Scarborough, also at two o'clock.

THE KITCHEN

Above: A set of jugs from the Brontë household, with illustrations from John Bunyan's The Pilgrim's Progress.
Below Left: In one of her misspelt diary fragments, dated 24 November 1834, Emily Brontë described a lively scene in the Parsonage kitchen: 'It is past Twelve o'clock Anne and I have not tidied ourselvs, done our bed work or done our lessons and we want to go out to play We are going to have for Dinner Boiled Beef Turnips, potato's and applepudding the Kitchin in a very untidy state…Taby said on my putting a pen in her face Ya pitter pottering there instead of pilling a potate I answered O Dear, ODear, O Dear I will directly with that I get up, take a Knife and begin pilling…'
Below Right: A tea urn which was used when the curates or parishioners came to tea. The urn fetched 17/6d at the 1861 sale.

'One night about the time when the cold sleet and dreary fogs of November are succeeded by the snow storms & high peircing nightwinds of confirmed winter we where all sitting round the warm blazing kitchen fire having just concluded a quarel with Taby concerning the propriety of lighting a candle…' Charlotte Brontë, *Tales of the Islanders*, 31 June 1829.

As children, the Brontës would gather round the kitchen fire to listen to their servant Tabby's dark tales of the Yorkshire moors. The sisters were expected to take their share of the household tasks, and the kitchen features in many of their surviving accounts of daily life at the Parsonage. After Aunt Branwell's death in 1842 Emily acted as housekeeper, helping in the kitchen and baking bread.

Following Patrick Brontë's death in 1861, the Parsonage became the home of the Revd. John Wade, who made several alterations to the house, the kitchen being the room most affected by the changes. A back kitchen, where the washing and heavier household work was carried out in the Brontës' time, was demolished to make way for a large kitchen extension, blocking the mullioned window which had formerly looked out towards the moors. The range was removed, and the old kitchen became a passage way to Wade's new dining room in the large gabled wing. Today the kitchen houses displays of furniture and utensils which belonged to the Brontë family, and a kitchen range of the correct period has been added to help recreate the room's original appearance.

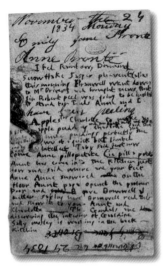

According to Elizabeth Gaskell, this room was originally 'a sort of flagged store-room', probably used for fuel, which could only be reached from the outside. Before her marriage in 1854 Charlotte converted the room into a study for her future husband, the Revd. Arthur Bell Nicholls, who in 1845 had come to assist her father as curate at Haworth Church. A fireplace was added to the room and the present doorway created into the entrance hall. Charlotte died within a year of her marriage, and Mr Nicholls remained at the Parsonage to care for the elderly Patrick Brontë and to assist in the performance of his pastoral duties. On Patrick's death in 1861, Mr Nicholls returned to his native Ireland, taking with him many mementoes of the Brontë family. He died in 1906 aged eighty-eight, having survived Charlotte by fifty-one years.

Describing her preparations for the room's conversion in a letter dated 22 May 1854, Charlotte wrote: '...I have been very busy stitching – the little new room is got into order now and the green and

Above: Arthur Bell Nicholls (1818-1906).
Right: Initially, Charlotte turned down Arthur Bell Nicholls' marriage proposal. Faced with Charlotte's rejection of him and her father's opposition, Nicholls decided to leave Haworth. This watch was bought by public subscription and given by the people of Haworth as a testimonial of respect to Nicholls. Eventually the situation was resolved, and Nicholls returned to Haworth.

white curtains are up – they exactly suit the papering and look neat and clean enough.' Three wallpaper samples were found in Charlotte's writing desk. A fourth sample, held in the New York Public Library, is accompanied by a note, authenticated by Elizabeth Gaskell, which describes it as being a 'Slip of the paper with which Charlotte Brontë papered her future husband's study, before they were married'.

Arthur Bell Nicholls was an extremely reserved man, and as so little is known about him, the room has been dedicated to Haworth Old Church, where he served as curate from 1845 to 1861.

Right: Several relics from the Old Church have been preserved, including this wooden board with the Lord's Prayer painted on it.

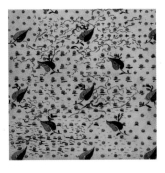

Left: Wallpaper sample found in Charlotte's desk.
Below: Wallpaper sample held in the New York Public Library.

THE SERVANT'S ROOM

Although we do not know exactly where the Parsonage inhabitants slept all of the time, there was always at least one live-in servant, and this was her bedroom. For thirty years the Brontës were served by a local woman, Tabby Aykroyd, who came to work at the Parsonage when she was in her fifties. Tabby was described in *The Life of Charlotte Brontë* as a 'thorough specimen of a Yorkshire woman of her class, in dialect, in appearance, and in character...Her words were far from flattery; but she would spare no deeds in the cause of those whom she kindly regarded.' Tabby must have been a comforting presence to the motherless

Above Left: Nancy Garrs (1803-1886) and her sister Sarah accompanied the Brontës from Thornton. They both stayed with the family for several years before leaving to get married. Sarah eventually emigrated to the United States. Nancy outlived all the Brontës (she attended the funerals of both Charlotte and Mr Brontë) and died in the Bradford workhouse at the age of 83.

Above Right: Martha Brown (1828-1880) came to the Parsonage in 1839, and remained with the family until Mr Brontë's death in 1861. Martha always kept in touch with Charlotte's husband, Arthur Bell Nicholls, after his return to Ireland, and even visited him there.

Top: At Patrick Brontë's death, Martha Brown was left the sum of thirty pounds, around three times her annual salary, 'as a token of regard for long and faithful services to me and my children'. Martha also possessed a treasured collection of drawings, inscribed copies of the novels, and other personal belongings from the Brontë household. This note by Patrick mentions a box of money - his gift to Martha Brown for a time of need.

Above Left: Mr Brontë wrote this testimonial for the Garrs sisters after Elizabeth Gaskell's The Life of Charlotte Brontë *described them as 'wasteful'.*

Above Right: Charlotte's letter to Amos Ingham, the Haworth surgeon, concerning Tabby's illness.

Brontë children. She became more of a family friend than a servant, and died at the age of eighty-four, just a few weeks before Charlotte in 1855. Martha Brown, the Sexton's daughter, came to the Parsonage at the age of eleven to assist Tabby. She also remained with the family for many years, and both women are buried in the churchyard, close to the Parsonage garden wall.

Originally this room was entered by means of an outside stone staircase. The original doorway has been partly uncovered. Also visible is part of a mullioned window which was probably blocked up in the Brontës' time, during alterations to the house.

CHARLOTTE'S ROOM

This was the main bedroom, used by different members of the family over the years, depending on who happened to be at home at any particular time. In the nineteenth century it was more common for people to share rooms and beds than it is today. The room was enlarged at the expense of the little room over the hall in 1850.

Initially, this was Patrick's and Maria's room. Maria Brontë died here on 15 September 1821 at the age of thirty-eight. During her painful illness (probably cancer) Mrs Brontë seldom complained and Elizabeth Gaskell described how she would beg her nurse to 'raise her bed to let her see her clean the grate, "because she did it as it was done in Cornwall".' After Mrs Brontë's death Aunt Branwell moved into this room and Patrick Brontë occupied the room opposite. At this time, Anne was still a baby and she slept here with her Aunt during much of her early childhood. When Aunt Branwell died in 1842, Emily returned from Brussels and remained at the Parsonage acting as housekeeper. Charlotte returned

Above: Few mementoes of the Brontës' mother Maria survive, but amongst them are a sampler, stitched when she was a girl, her copy of James Thomson's Seasons, *and her china smelling salts bottle. The first portrait of Maria is by an unknown artist. The copy, painted by Charlotte when she was fourteen years old, makes her mother look more attractive.*

Portrait said to be of Charlotte, based on George Richmond's famous portrait, and painted after her death by J.H.Thompson, a friend of Branwell's who knew Charlotte personally.

permanently from Brussels in early 1844 and may have taken over the room then. Anne left Thorp Green in June 1845 and probably shared with either Charlotte or Emily from this point onwards. After the deaths of her sisters, Charlotte occupied this room, moving out occasionally if guests such as Elizabeth Gaskell came to stay. When Charlotte married, she and her husband, Arthur Bell Nicholls shared the room. Charlotte died here on 31 March 1855, at the age of thirty-eight. Elizabeth Gaskell described how the gravely ill Charlotte overheard her husband praying beside her: 'Oh!' she whispered forth, 'I am not going to die, am I? He will not separate us, we have been so happy.'

Left: Bonnet worn by Charlotte.
Below Left: An unflattering self-caricature by Charlotte, 6 March 1843.
Below: Section from one of Charlotte's last letters, written in pencil from her sick-bed to her friend Amelia Taylor.

Below: Silhouette portrait of Aunt Branwell, her smelling salts bottle with the monogram 'EB', the wooden pattens or overshoes which she used to wear to protect her feet from the cold stone floors of the Parsonage, and her japanned dressing case, which she left to Branwell in her will. Aunt Branwell had sacrificed a comfortable life in Penzance to look after her sister's six small children. It was her financial support which made Charlotte and Emily's trip to Brussels possible, and her legacy to the three sisters which funded the publication of their Poems *in 1846.*

Above: These four dresses are said to have been worn by Charlotte. In Jane Eyre, *Charlotte created a heroine who was as 'small, obscure, plain and little' as she perceived herself to be. From her surviving dresses, we can estimate that Charlotte was less than five feet tall and possibly as small as 4' 9" or 4' 10" tall (1m 45cm). She was described by people who knew her as 'very small', 'tiny', 'childlike' and 'diminutive', and her sense of being 'different' both physically and intellectually informs her writing.*

Most of the costume items in the collection belonged to Charlotte. As a young girl, her clothes sense was described by Ellen as very old-fashioned. Later in life, she favoured simple, elegant clothes.

This little room is particularly associated with the Brontës as children, and later was Emily's bedroom. Originally it would have been wider, with room for a full sized bed across the window, as shown in Emily's diary paper sketch, but it was affected by the enlargement of Charlotte's room in 1850. According to Elizabeth Gaskell, the servants called the room the 'children's study' because it was here that the young children would act out their plays and write in their handmade little books. The room may have been used by Branwell at some point as the only boy, but is usually associated with Emily.

Top Right: Emily's 1845 diary paper sketch shows herself writing in her bedroom with her devoted mastiff Keeper lying at her feet. The chest and little stool shown in the sketch are displayed in the room.

Middle Right: Detail from Branwell's 'Battel Book' of 1827 drawn when he was eight years old.

Bottom Right: Keeper, drawn from life by Emily, 24 April 1838.

Mrs Gaskell described how Keeper was punished by Emily for stealing upstairs and sleeping on the clean 'delicate white counterpanes' covering the beds. Martha Brown told Mrs Gaskell how Keeper and Mr Brontë walked 'first side by side' at Emily's funeral, and how the dog had 'howled pitifully' at Emily's bedroom door for many days afterwards. In a letter of June 1849, Charlotte recalled how, 'Emily's large house-dog…lay at the side of her dying-bed, and followed her funeral to the vault, lying in the pew couched at our feet while the burial service was being read…', and how, over six months after her death, he still made a daily visit to 'Emily's little bed-room', looking for his mistress.

MR BRONTË'S BEDROOM

After the death of his wife in 1821, Patrick Brontë left the room they had shared and moved into the bedroom across the landing, which remained his for the rest of his life. Patrick had lived through periods of Luddite and Chartist violence, to which clergymen often fell victim, and as a result would place a loaded pistol beside his bed at night, discharging the bullet by firing it from his bedroom window across the graveyard every morning.

In later years, Branwell's addiction to alcohol and opium made him a danger both to himself and his family. Mary Robinson, an early biographer, was told that on one occasion Branwell, stupefied with alcohol, set his bed on fire and was rescued by Emily. Whether true or not, it was the fear of such incidents which led Mr Brontë to share his room with Branwell, in order to watch over him. Elizabeth Gaskell, writing of this period in the Brontës' lives, said of Branwell: 'For some time before his death he had attacks of delirium

Above: 'A Parody', Branwell Brontë's last surviving drawing, a grim pen and ink sketch showing himself being summoned from sleep by Death.

tremens of the most frightful character; he slept in his father's room, and he would sometimes declare that either he or his father should be dead before morning …In the mornings young Brontë would saunter out, saying, with a drunkard's incontinence of speech, "The poor old man and I have had a terrible night of it; he does his best – the poor old man! but it's all over with me."' It was in this room that Branwell died at the age of thirty-one on Sunday 24 September 1848, repenting the fact that in all his life he had 'done nothing either great or good'.

In 1860 Elizabeth Gaskell, accompanied by her daughter Meta, paid her last visit to see Mr Brontë, who was by this time confined to bed: 'we were taken into his bedroom; where everything was delicately clean and white, and there he was sitting propped up in bed in a clean nightgown, with a clean towel laid just for his hands to play upon…' Mr Brontë, having outlived his wife and children, died here on 7 June 1861, at the age of eighty-four.

Left: Very little of the Brontës' bedroom furniture, and none of the original beds, have survived. In an attempt to recreate a room setting, a reproduction bed was made locally. Based on the sketch by Branwell, the bed is a half tester, a style commonly in use at this period, and also shown in this tiny watercolour illustration by Charlotte.

Above Left: A nightshirt worn by Charlotte Brontë, and Mr Brontë's nightcap.
Above Right: A washstand used in the Brontë household.
Left: This multicoloured patchwork quilt is believed to have been worked by the Brontë sisters. The quilt, which was never completed, was included in a sale of Brontë relics held at Sotheby's in 1898.

BRANWELL'S STUDIO

For much of the time this room would have been used as a bedroom. At one period it served as a studio for Branwell, who had trained with the Leeds artist William Robinson, and who hoped to become a professional portrait painter. During Elizabeth Gaskell's visit to the Parsonage in 1853 this room was used as a bedroom by Charlotte. In the 1870s, when Wade extended the house, the window of this room was blocked up, so that the room became a passage-way to the new wing.

Patrick Branwell Brontë occupied the privileged position of only boy in the family, with all expectations centred on him. His weakness of character and lack of application meant that he failed first in his chosen profession of artist, and eventually proved himself to be unemployable. In 1843 Branwell became tutor to the son of Mr and Mrs Robinson at Thorp Green Hall, near York, where his sister Anne was employed as governess. In July 1845 Branwell was dismissed from his post, apparently because of a love affair with Mrs Lydia Robinson. Branwell could not recover from this final blow, and turned increasingly to alcohol and opium. Inevitably his addiction ruined his health and contributed to his death from tuberculosis at the age of thirty-one in September 1848.

Following his funeral service, Branwell's life and death were summed up by his sister Charlotte: 'Branwell was his father's and his sisters' pride and hope in boyhood, but since manhood the case has been otherwise. It has been our lot to see him take a wrong bent...and now to behold the sudden early obscure close of what might have been a noble career.'

Above: A self-portrait by Branwell Brontë, c. 1840.
Below: During his time as a portrait painter in Bradford, Branwell lodged with Mr and Mrs Isaac Kirby at Fountain Street. These portraits are believed to have been painted to cover the rent which Branwell could not afford to pay.

Above Left: Margaret Hartley, the young niece of Mr and Mrs Kirby, met Branwell at their home in Bradford and had her portrait painted by him.
Above Right: Branwell's portrait of John Brown (1804-1855), the Haworth sexton and stonemason who lived in the house adjoining the Sunday School. Brown was Worshipful Master of the Masonic Lodge of the Three Graces, into which Branwell was initiated in 1836. John Brown's daughter, Martha, was for many years a servant in the Brontë household.

Top Right: *William Thomas (b.1814) was the son of William Thomas senior, a wine and spirit merchant of Haworth. According to oral tradition in the Thomas family, the portrait was painted by Branwell in lieu of debts.*

Right: *A portrait of John Ogden Wood (1831-1896) by Branwell Brontë. The portrait, dated 4 April 1836, shows the young son of William Wood, the Haworth cabinet-maker who made several items of furniture for the Brontës, some of which are still to be seen in the Parsonage.*

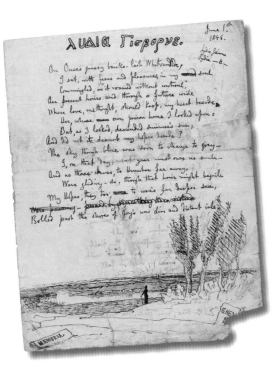

Above: *The manuscript of Branwell's poem to Mrs Robinson, 'Lydia Gisborne', dated 1 June 1846.*
Right: *This wooden armchair is believed to be Branwell's favourite chair from the Black Bull.*

ABOUT THE COLLECTION

fter the death of Patrick Brontë in 1861 the household contents of Haworth Parsonage were sold at auction. As the Brontës' fame spread, souvenir hunters made visits to Haworth, and people who had been connected with the family, or who had purchased items at the 1861 sale, were persuaded to part with their treasures. In this way the Brontë relics began to be dispersed. It was in an attempt to halt this dispersal that the Brontë Society was founded in 1893.

By far the largest collections of Brontëana were those owned by Charlotte's widower Arthur Bell Nicholls, her close friend Ellen Nussey, and the family servant Martha Brown. Martha possessed many personal belongings of the Brontës and was happy to show her collection to interested visitors. Although she did sell selected items, presumably on occasions of financial necessity, she was reluctant to part with her mementoes, and it was not until after her death in

Top Right: Catalogue for the Sale at Haworth Parsonage, held on 1 and 2 October 1861.
Above: Martha Brown.
Right: Catalogue of the Sale at Ellen Nussey's home, Moor Lane House, held in 1898 after Ellen's death.

Right: Arthur Bell Nicholls.
Below: A sample of Charlotte Brontë's handwriting authenticated by Arthur Bell Nicholls, 11 January 1861.

1880 that Martha's collection was dispersed. In accordance with the terms of her will, the collection was divided amongst her five sisters, all struggling to raise families on limited incomes, and all eagerly sought out by collectors. In 1886 Martha's recently widowed sister, Ann Binns, was obliged to sell her share of the inheritance and the resulting auction was one of the first sales of Brontëana.

By the time of her death in 1897 Ellen Nussey had already parted with her large collection of Charlotte Brontë letters. Ellen's later years were troubled by

Left: Thomas James Wise.
Below: Henry Houston Bonnell.
Bottom: Sir James Roberts.

collectors and biographers all eager to make use of her letters. When the respected bibliographer and collector Thomas J. Wise offered to buy the letters, giving an assurance that they would eventually be deposited in a national collection, it seemed like the perfect solution. Wise also acquired many of the Brontës' manuscripts from Arthur Bell Nicholls. Using the Brontë biographer Clement Shorter as his agent, Nicholls had been tracked down to the relative obscurity of his home in Ireland. Trusting that he was safeguarding the future of the precious manuscripts (he too was under the impression that the material would be bequeathed to the nation), Nicholls sold a large collection of manuscripts, including many of the famous Brontë 'little books' which, unbeknown to him, were soon being lavishly bound and sold by Wise to collectors around the world, 'doubtless for his own commercial advantage', as Shorter commented in a letter. Wise did not manage to acquire everything, and Brontëana which Arthur Bell Nicholls had been unwilling to part with during his lifetime was sold at Sotheby's in 1907 after his death the previous year. Although unable to compete with wealthy collectors, the Brontë Society managed to acquire several items in this sale and a subsequent one in 1914.

In 1934 Thomas J. Wise was exposed as a forger and a manufacturer of counterfeit first editions, but by that time the damage to Brontë scholarship had been done. Manuscripts were scattered far and wide, with those by Branwell often passed off as the work of his more collectable sister Charlotte. In fact by the time of Wise's death in 1937, when his personal collection of books and literary artefacts was sold to the British Library, shockingly few Brontë manuscripts remained, considering the huge amount of material which had passed through his hands.

In 1928 Sir James Roberts, a local man who had made a fortune in the textile industry, provided the money which enabled the Brontë Society to achieve its ambition of acquiring Haworth Parsonage, the Brontës' former home. The Museum Collection, previously exhibited in a crowded room above the Yorkshire Penny Bank, was transferred there. The Collection, augmented by generous gifts and loans from local people, was enriched at this time by the addition of a large collection of Brontëana which came as the gift of the American collector, Henry Houston Bonnell, who had died the previous year. The acquisition of both the Parsonage and the Bonnell Collection greatly enhanced the reputation of the Brontë Society, and today the Museum continues to add to its unrivalled collection of Brontëana.

TREASURES FROM THE COLLECTION

T he Brontë Parsonage Museum has the largest collection of Brontë material anywhere in the world. The collection includes a wide range of items, including letters, manuscripts, paintings and drawings, costume, jewellery, furniture and personal memorabilia. There are also unusual items such as Anne's collection of pebbles gathered in Scarborough, where she is buried, and the brass dog collars belonging to Anne's dog Flossie and Emily's dog Keeper. Many objects in the museum's collection are of little intrinsic value or rarity; they illustrate middle class life in the first half of the nineteenth century. Their particular importance lies in their association value and the insight they provide into the lives of three famous authors.

Above: Anne's collection of pebbles from Scarborough.
Left: Portrait of Anne by Charlotte, 17 April 1833

Top: Flossie's and Keeper's brass collars.
Above: Anne's dog Flossie, an undated watercolour previously attributed to Charlotte but now believed to be by Emily.

Right: Part of Anne Brontë's last letter, 5 April 1849.
Anne was gravely ill with consumption and wrote to Ellen Nussey to ask if she would be willing to travel with her and Charlotte to Scarborough on the Yorkshire coast. It was hoped that the sea air might cure her. The letter is 'crossed', with the lines written both horizontally and vertically, a common practice at the time to save on postal costs. She wrote: 'I wish it would please God to spare me not only for Papa's and Charlotte's sakes, but because I long to do some good in the world before I leave it. I have many schemes in my head for future practise – humble and limited indeed – but still I should not like them all to come to nothing, and myself to have lived to so little purpose.' Anne died in Scarborough a few weeks later, on 28 May 1849.

Above: Emily's Writing Desk and Contents.
Charlotte, Emily and Anne each owned a portable folding writing desk like this one. Charlotte's and Emily's desks survived with their contents intact, though Anne's was empty. Amongst the items in Emily's desk were five reviews of Wuthering Heights, *a programme from a concert in Brussels, various pens and steel nibs, and an ivory-handled brass seal and sealing wax. There was also a letter of 15 February 1848 from Emily's publisher, T.C. Newby, addressed to 'Dear Sir' and discussing arrangements for the author's second novel. An envelope into which the letter fits exactly is addressed in the same hand to 'Ellis Bell, Esq'. If the letter and envelope do indeed belong together, it is possible that Emily was working on another novel prior to her death. The fate of any such manuscript is unknown.*

Right: Diary paper by Emily and Anne, 24 November 1834.
At intervals of a few years, Emily and Anne made informal written records of what was happening to them on a particular day, usually Emily's birthday, and what were their hopes for the future. It presents a fascinating and vivid mixture of reality and fantasy. In one sentence from the 1834 paper, Emily moves without pause from 'The Gondals are discovering the interior of Gaaldine' to 'Sally mosley is washing in the back Kitchin'.

Right: Samplers by Maria and Elizabeth Brontë.
The only surviving relics of the two eldest Brontë children, who died in 1825, are these faded samplers, stitched by Maria at the age of eight and Elizabeth at the age of seven. There are also samplers by Charlotte, Emily, Anne, Mrs Brontë and Aunt Branwell in the museum's collection.
Below: The Young Men's Magazine, August 1830 by Charlotte.
One of the early 'little books' made by the Brontës as children, reproduced actual size. It has been set out to look like a real book, with a contents page and headings, and is sewn together.

Above Left: Christening Mug which belonged to Emily.
Above Right: Grasper by Emily, January 1834.
Like her watercolour of her later dog Keeper, this sketch of Grasper was taken from life. Of the few surviving drawings by Emily, the majority are studies of animals and birds, reflecting her love of the natural world.

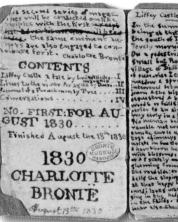

Below: These patterned cloth boots with leather soles and toes were worn by Charlotte. They are just 234 mm in length. Charlotte had similarly delicate hands.

Bottom Right: Charlotte's Wedding Bonnet.
Charlotte's delicate wedding bonnet and veil are poignant reminders of the brief happiness which she shared with her husband Arthur Bell Nicholls before her death, less than a year after their marriage. The bonnet has faded from its original green and white. On her wedding day, villagers described Charlotte as looking like 'a little snowdrop'. Charlotte's white muslin wedding dress was destroyed at Mr Nicholls' request after his death but a copy, now in a private collection, was made at a later date.

Bottom Left: Charlotte's Going Away Dress.
This dress is said to have been worn by Charlotte on her honeymoon tour in Ireland. Like Jane Eyre, the 'plain' heroine, Charlotte preferred simple, understated clothes, and this is reflected in her choice of honeymoon outfit. The dress, which is actually a separate bodice and skirt, has faded to a brownish mauve from its original striped lavender colour.

Above Left: Charlotte's Writing Desk and Contents.
Charlotte's desk contained writing materials such as ink bottles, sealing wax, blotting paper and enamelled sealing wafers printed with phrases such as 'In answer to yours' and 'Excuse haste'. There was one quill pen in the desk, and over a hundred steel nibs for the wooden handled pens which were introduced in the 1840s.

Above Right: Charlotte's Paint Box.
Like her sisters and brother, Charlotte was keen on painting and drawing. She was once ambitious to be a professional artist and two of her pencil drawings - of Kirkstall Abbey and Bolton Abbey - were exhibited at the Royal Northern Society for the Encouragement of the Fine Arts in Leeds in 1834. In later life Charlotte turned down an invitation from her publishers to illustrate a new edition of Jane Eyre, *explaining that her ability was limited. This paint box still has its original solid cakes of paint and dishes for mixing colours.*

Right: Letter from Mr Nicholls informing Ellen Nussey of his wife Charlotte's death, 31 March 1855.
On the previous day Mr Brontë had written to Ellen warning her that Charlotte was 'on the verge of the grave' and that Mr Nicholls was so distressed that 'he is not so sufficiently strong and composed as to be able to write.' This letter is brief and painful to read. It opens with these words: 'Mr Brontë's letter would prepare you for the sad intelligence I have to communicate – our dear Charlotte is no more – She died last night of exhaustion.'

A MAP OF BRONTË COUNTRY

Inset map (British Isles):

BELFAST
DRUMBALLY-RONEY
COWAN BRIDGE
SCARBOROUGH
HAWORTH
CAMBRIDGE
LONDON
PENZANCE
BRUSSELS
PARIS •

Main map:

Little Ouseburn
Thorp Green

A61
A1
A59
A59
HARROGATE

SKIPTON
A629
A65
OTLEY
A658
A61
A58
A1
YOR

Lothersdale
Stonegappe
ILKLEY
A64

KEIGHLEY
A650
BINGLEY
A629
Rawdon
Upperwood House
A642

HAWORTH
Stanbury •
B6144
LEEDS
A63

Oxenhope
Thornton
BRADFORD
A6033
B6145
A629
A650
M621
A6110
A672
A646
A6036
A641
M606
Gomersal
Red House
Birstall
Rydings
Brookroyd
M1

HALIFAX
Southowram
Law Hill
Hartshead

Luddenden Foot
A58
Mirfield
Blake Hall
Roe Head
A644
DEWSBURY

Sowerby Bridge •
M62
M1

A62
HUDDERSFIELD
A629

| 0 | 5 | 10 |
miles

| 0 | 5 | 10 |
kilometres

42

Inset map (HAWORTH TODAY):

WEST LANE
OLD WHITE LION
TOURIST INFORMATION OFFICE
CAR PARK
KING'S ARMS
MAIN STREET
SUNDAY SCHOOL
BRONTË PARSONAGE MUSEUM
ST MICHAEL & ALL ANGELS CHURCH
BLACK BULL

HAWORTH TODAY

THE BRONTËS: A BRIEF CHRONOLOGY

1777 17 March	**Patrick Brontë born at Emdale, County Down, Ireland**	*1816 21 April*	**Charlotte Brontë born at Thornton. Baptised at Thornton on 29 June**
1783 15 April	**Maria Branwell born at Penzance, Cornwall**	*1817 26 June*	**Patrick Branwell Brontë born at Thornton. Baptised at Thornton on 23 July**
1802	Patrick Brontë entered St John's College, Cambridge	*1818 30 July*	**Emily Jane Brontë born at Thornton. Baptised at Thornton on 20 August**
1806	Patrick Brontë ordained as a clergyman in the Church of England	*1820 17 January*	**Anne Brontë born at Thornton. Baptised at Thornton on 25 March**
1806-1809	Patrick Brontë Curate at Wethersfield, Essex	*1820 February*	Patrick Brontë appointed Perpetual Curate at Haworth
1809 January-December	Patrick Brontë Curate at Wellington, Shropshire	*1820 April*	Brontës moved to Haworth
1809 December-1811	Patrick Brontë Curate at Dewsbury, Yorkshire	*1821 15 September*	Mrs Maria Brontë died and was buried in Haworth Church; her sister, Miss Elizabeth Branwell came from Penzance to look after the family
1811-1815	Patrick Brontë Minister at Hartshead-cum-Clifton, Yorkshire		
1812	Maria Branwell visited her uncle, John Fennell, Headmaster of Woodhouse Grove School, near Bradford, where Patrick was an examiner in the Classics	*1824 July*	Maria and Elizabeth went to the Clergy Daughters' School at Cowan Bridge, Kirkby Lonsdale. They were joined in August by Charlotte and in November by Emily
1812 29 December	Patrick Brontë married Maria Branwell at Guiseley Church, near Leeds	*1825 6 May*	Maria died at Haworth, having left school due to ill-health on 14 February
1814	Maria Brontë born at Hartshead. Baptised at Hartshead on 23 April	*1825 1 June*	Charlotte and Emily withdrawn from school
1815 8 February	Elizabeth Brontë born at Hartshead. Baptised at Thornton on 26 August	*1825 15 June*	Elizabeth died at Haworth, having left school due to ill-health on 31 May
1815	Patrick Brontë appointed Perpetual Curate at Thornton near Bradford	*1825*	Tabitha Aykroyd came as a servant to the Parsonage

1831 January	Charlotte went to Miss Wooler's school at Roe Head, Mirfield, where she met her life-long friends, Ellen Nussey and Mary Taylor
1832 June	Charlotte left Roe Head to teach her sisters at home
1835 July	Charlotte returned to Roe Head as a teacher taking Emily as a free pupil; Emily stayed only briefly, Anne taking her place and staying till December 1837
1838 June	Branwell set up as a portrait painter in Bradford, but returned home in debt, May 1839
1838 September	Emily worked as teacher at Miss Patchett's school at Law Hill, near Halifax, where she stayed approximately six months
1838 December	Charlotte left her teaching post at Miss Wooler's school
1839 April-December	Anne worked as governess for Mrs Ingham at Blake Hall, Mirfield
1839 May-July	Charlotte worked as governess for Mrs Sidgwick at Stonegappe, Lothersdale
1839 August	William Weightman appointed Curate at Haworth Church
1839 September	Charlotte and Ellen Nussey took a holiday at Easton Farm, Bridlington
1840 January-June	Branwell worked as tutor for Mr Postlethwaite at Broughton-in-Furness
1840 May	Anne worked as governess for Mrs Robinson at Thorp Green Hall, Little Ouseburn, near York
1840 October	Branwell worked as clerk on the new Leeds-Manchester railway at Sowerby Bridge, Halifax
1841 March-December	Charlotte worked as governess for Mrs White at Upperwood House, Rawdon
1841 April	Branwell promoted and sent as clerk-in-charge to Luddenden Foot, near Halifax
1842 February	Charlotte and Emily travelled to Brussels to enrol at the Pensionnat Heger
1842 April	Branwell dismissed from Luddenden Foot for negligence in keeping the accounts
1842 6 September	William Weightman died, aged 26, and was buried in Haworth Church
1842 29 October	Miss Elizabeth Branwell died, aged 66, and was buried in Haworth Church. Charlotte and Emily recalled from Brussels on the death of their aunt
1843 January	Charlotte returned to Brussels. Emily remained at the Parsonage as housekeeper. Branwell accompanied Anne back to Thorp Green as tutor to Edmund Robinson
1844 January	Charlotte finally left Brussels and returned home
1845 May	Arthur Bell Nicholls appointed Curate at Haworth Church
1845 June	Anne resigned from her post at Thorp Green
1845 July	Branwell dismissed from Thorp Green. Charlotte stayed with Ellen Nussey at Hathersage, Derbyshire
1846 May	***Poems* by Currer, Ellis and Acton Bell published by Aylott and Jones at the sisters' expense**

1846 June	Charlotte completed *The Professor* which was rejected by several publishers. By July Emily had completed *Wuthering Heights* and Anne *Agnes Grey*
1846 August	Charlotte accompanied Patrick Brontë to Manchester for a cataract operation and began writing *Jane Eyre*
1847 19 October	**Jane Eyre published by Smith, Elder & Co. under Charlotte's pseudonym, Currer Bell, to instant acclaim**
1847 December	**Wuthering Heights and Agnes Grey published together by Thomas Cautley Newby under Emily and Anne's pseudonyms, Ellis and Acton Bell**
1848 June	**The Tenant of Wildfell Hall, Anne's second novel, published by Thomas Cautley Newby**
1848 July	Charlotte and Anne travelled to London to prove to Smith, Elder & Co. that they were separate individuals. Newby had claimed that all the Bells were a single author
1848 24 September	**Branwell died (probably of tuberculosis), aged 31, and was buried in Haworth Church**
1848 19 December	**Emily died of tuberculosis, aged 30, and was buried in Haworth Church**
1849 28 May	**Anne died of tuberculosis, aged 29, and was buried in St. Mary's churchyard at Scarborough where she had gone in the hope of a sea cure**
1849 June	Charlotte stayed in Filey and at Easton Farm, Bridlington
1849 26 October	**Shirley published by Smith, Elder & Co. under Charlotte's pseudonym, Currer Bell**
1849 December	Charlotte stayed with George Smith's family in London, where she met Thackeray and Harriet Martineau
1850 March	Charlotte visited Sir James Kay-Shuttleworth at Gawthorpe Hall, near Burnley
1850 June	Charlotte stayed again with the Smiths in London, dining with Thackeray and having her portrait painted by George Richmond
1850 July	Charlotte visited Edinburgh with George Smith
1850 August	Charlotte stayed with the Kay-Shuttleworths at Briery Close, Windermere, where she met Elizabeth Gaskell
1850 December	Charlotte visited Harriet Martineau at The Knoll, Ambleside
1851 May-June	Charlotte visited London, saw the Great Exhibition and attended Thackeray's lectures
1851 June	Charlotte stayed with Elizabeth Gaskell at Plymouth Grove, Manchester
1852 June	Charlotte stayed alone at Filey, East Yorkshire, and visited Anne's grave at Scarborough
1852 December	Arthur Bell Nicholls proposed marriage to Charlotte but was rejected due to her father's objections

1853 January	**Charlotte visited London for the last time.** *Villette* **published by Smith, Elder & Co. under Charlotte's pseudonym, Currer Bell**
1853 April	Charlotte stayed a week with Elizabeth Gaskell at Plymouth Grove, Manchester
1853 May	Arthur Bell Nicholls resigned his curacy at Haworth. In August he transferred to Kirk Smeaton, Pontefract
1853 September	Elizabeth Gaskell spent four days at Haworth Parsonage
1854 January	Arthur Bell Nicholls stayed with Mr Grant, Curate at Oxenhope, and met Charlotte several times
1854 April	Patrick Brontë withdrew his objections to the marriage and Charlotte's engagement to Arthur Bell Nicholls was announced
1854 June	Arthur Bell Nicholls resumed his duties as Curate at Haworth
1854 29 June	Charlotte and Arthur Bell Nicholls married in Haworth Church by the Reverend Sutcliffe Sowden. Miss Wooler gave her away and Ellen Nussey acted as bridesmaid
1854 July	Charlotte and Arthur Bell Nicholls went on honeymoon to Ireland and visited Nicholls' relations
1855 January	Charlotte and Arthur Bell Nicholls visited the Kay-Shuttleworths at Gawthorpe Hall. Charlotte caught a chill from walking on wet grass from which she never fully recovered
1855 17 February	Tabitha Aykroyd, the beloved servant of the Brontë family, died, aged 84
1855 31 March	**Charlotte Brontë Nicholls died, in the early stages of pregnancy, aged 38**
1855 June	Patrick Brontë wrote to Elizabeth Gaskell suggesting she should write Charlotte's biography
1857 March	*The Life of Charlotte Brontë* by Elizabeth Gaskell published by Smith, Elder & Co.
1857 June	*The Professor*, **Charlotte's first novel, published for the first time by Smith, Elder & Co. with a preface by Arthur Bell Nicholls**
1861 7 June	**Patrick Brontë died, aged 84. Arthur Bell Nicholls left the Parsonage and returned to Ireland**
1861 October	Sale of the household effects of Haworth Parsonage
1878	Patrick Brontë's successor, the Revd. John Wade, added a gabled wing to the Parsonage
1879	Haworth Church demolished, except for the tower, and rebuilt on the same site
1880 19 January	Martha Brown the Brontës' servant, died, aged 52
1893 16 December	The Brontë Society founded at a meeting in Bradford Town Hall
1895 18 May	The Brontë Museum opened in the upper floor of the Yorkshire Penny Bank, Haworth
1897 26 November	Ellen Nussey, Charlotte's life-long friend, died, aged 80
1906 2 December	Arthur Bell Nicholls, Charlotte's husband, died at Banagher, Ireland, aged 88
1928 4 August	Haworth Parsonage opened to the public as the Brontë Parsonage Museum, having been bought by Sir James Roberts and presented to the Brontë Society

A FAMILY HISTORY

In 1820 Patrick Brontë was appointed as incumbent of Haworth, and arrived in the township with his Cornish-born wife, Maria, and their six children. Although Haworth remained the family's home for the rest of their lives, and the moorland setting had a profound influence on the writing of Charlotte, Emily and Anne Brontë, the family history began not in Yorkshire, but in Ireland, where Patrick, the first of ten children, was born in County Down, on 17 March 1777. Driven by ambition, Patrick left his humble origins far behind and was accepted at St. John's College, Cambridge, where his original family name of Brunty was dropped in favour of the more impressive sounding 'Brontë'. The hard work and commitment which had won him a place at Cambridge carried him through several curacies, mainly in the North of England, until he arrived at Haworth. By this time Patrick Brontë was a published author of poetry and fiction, so that his children grew up accustomed to the sight of books carrying their name on the Parsonage shelves.

On 15 September 1821, Mrs Brontë died of cancer, and her unmarried sister, Elizabeth Branwell, came to take charge of the running of the Parsonage, exchanging her comfortable home in Penzance for the harsh climate of a bleak northern township. In 1824 the four eldest daughters made their first venture into the world outside Haworth, to attend the Clergy Daughters' School at Cowan Bridge, near Kirkby Lonsdale. The experience, which provided Charlotte with a model for the infamous Lowood School in her novel *Jane Eyre*, ended in tragedy when her eldest sister, Maria, was sent home in ill-health. Maria died at the Parsonage in May 1825, aged eleven. Ten-year-

Right: The house at Thornton where the four famous Brontë children were born. Below: Charlotte's drawing of Roe Head School, c.1831-1832.

old Elizabeth was returned home shortly after, only to die at Haworth on 15 June. For the next few years the surviving children remained at home together, creating a rich imaginary world, sparked by their father's gift to Branwell of a set of toy soldiers. Because of the important role education had played in his own life, Patrick encouraged his children in their pursuit of knowledge. Any books that came their way were eagerly devoured, and the children produced their own tiny illustrated books, designed to be small enough for the toy soldiers, with minuscule handwriting to deter the prying eyes of the Parsonage adults.

Their father's lack of a private income meant that the sisters needed to acquire the accomplishments that would enable them to earn a living as governesses – the only career option socially acceptable for genteel young ladies with no fortune. To this end, Charlotte was sent to Miss Wooler's school at Roe Head, Mirfield, in 1831. There she met her lifelong friends, Ellen Nussey and Mary Taylor. She eventually returned to the school as a teacher, taking first Emily then Anne as pupils. Branwell, the only boy of the family, when not receiving lessons from his father, was often left to his own devices. Eventually his brilliant conversation earned him what Elizabeth Gaskell considered 'the undesirable distinction of having his company recommended by the landlord of the Black Bull to any chance traveller who might happen to feel solitary or dull over his liquor.' Branwell took art lessons in Leeds, but a plan to apply to the Royal Academy of Arts in London never came off, and after a short stint as a professional portrait painter in Bradford, Branwell was back in Haworth, in debt.

In 1839, after one brief attempt as a teacher at Miss Patchett's School at Law Hill, Halifax, where she was reported to have told her pupils she much

Left: Mary Taylor, Charlotte's lifelong friend from Roe Head, photographed in old age. Below: An early letter from Charlotte to Ellen Nussey, 5 September 1832.

preferred the school dog to any of them, Emily was also back at Haworth. Although often unhappy, Anne seems to have been the best able to cope with life as a governess. Her second post, as governess to the Robinsons at Thorp Green Hall, near York, lasted five years, and her success enabled her to secure the post of tutor to the family's only son for Branwell. Branwell was proving to be a cause for concern – an earlier post as tutor, and a position as clerk-in-charge on the Leeds-Manchester railway, had both ended ignominiously, and this new situation was to be no exception. Anne decided to leave her employment at Thorp Green and came back to Haworth in June 1845, followed shortly after by Branwell, dismissed in disgrace for 'proceedings bad beyond expression' – allegedly a love affair with his employer's wife.

In an attempt to escape the hated life of a governess, the sisters planned to set up a school of their own at the Parsonage. In order to acquire the language skills which would attract pupils and secure the school's success, Charlotte and Emily spent a year studying in Brussels, funded by their aunt. It was Aunt Branwell's death in 1842 which brought the sisters back to Haworth. Emily remained at the Parsonage as housekeeper, while Charlotte returned to Brussels. Charlotte returned to Haworth permanently in 1844, suffering the pains of unrequited love for her teacher, Monsieur Heger. The school project foundered when a prospectus was circulated but pupils could not be found.

The sisters had continued to write, and in 1846 Charlotte, Emily and Anne used part of Aunt Branwell's legacy to finance the publication of their poems, concealing their true identities under the pseudonyms Currer, Ellis and Acton Bell. *Poems* was published by Aylott and Jones, but despite some favourable reviews only two copies of the book were sold. Undeterred, the sisters absorbed themselves in their next literary venture – novel writing.

Charlotte's first attempt at writing a novel for publication, *The Professor*, was rejected by several publishing houses, before it arrived at the offices of Smith, Elder & Co. Although the firm declined to accept the novel, their response was sufficiently encouraging for Charlotte to send them her next work, *Jane Eyre*, begun in a dreary Manchester lodging while nursing her father back to health after a cataract operation. If *Poems* ranks amongst the great failures in publishing history, then *Jane Eyre* must count as one of the great successes.

George Smith accepted the book without hesitation, and the novel appeared on 19 October 1847. *Wuthering Heights* and *Agnes Grey* had already been accepted by the London publisher, Thomas Cautley Newby, and appeared as a three-volume set in December 1847. Following the success of *Jane Eyre*, the publication of two further 'Bell' novels fuelled speculation about the gender and identity of the authors.

The publication of Anne's second novel, *The Tenant of Wildfell Hall*, forced Charlotte and Anne to reveal their separate identities to George Smith, as the unscrupulous Newby tried to pass off the work of his author as being by the more successful Currer Bell. The two sisters travelled to London in July 1848 and confronted the astonished George Smith in his Cornhill office. Charlotte and Anne, staying quietly at the Chapter Coffee House, resisted Smith's attempts to show them off, but they did find themselves being escorted to the opera, the National Gallery and the Royal Academy of Arts.

Charlotte's pleasure in her new-found success turned out to be shortlived. Branwell, who had increasingly fallen back on alcohol and opium for solace, had been ailing all summer. Tuberculosis was gaining a rapid hold on his abused frame. He died suddenly on Sunday 24 September 1848, aged thirty-one, with the whole family at his death-bed. While Charlotte was still reeling from the shock of Branwell's death, it became apparent that Emily and Anne were ill. In fact Emily was also dying from tuberculosis, and never left the house again after Branwell's funeral. Refusing to admit she was ill, she dragged herself out of bed every morning and continued to carry out her share of the household chores. Her death came at the age of thirty, three months after her brother's, on 19 December 1848. All Charlotte's concern was now directed towards her last-surviving sister, who seemed unable to shake off her cold. A lung specialist, called in to examine Anne shortly after Emily's death, confirmed Charlotte's

Left: William Smith Williams, the reader at Smith, Elder & Co. who corresponded regularly with Charlotte.
Below: George Smith as a young man.
Bottom: Anne Brontë's grave in the churchyard of St. Mary's, Scarborough.

worst fear, that she was likely to lose this last, much-loved sister.

Anne submitted to all the futile treatments then available, but any benefit proved to be temporary. In January 1849 Charlotte wrote: 'Anne cannot study now, she can scarcely read; she occupies Emily's chair – she does not get well.' Anne was anxious to try a sea cure, and on 24 May, accompanied by Charlotte and Ellen Nussey, she set out for Scarborough, a place she had loved from her summers there with the Robinson family. It was in Scarborough that Anne died, just four days later, on 28 May 1849, aged twenty-nine years. To spare her father the anguish of yet another family funeral, Charlotte took the decision to bury her sister in Scarborough, where she was laid to rest in the churchyard of St. Mary's, high above the town. Stunned by the tragedies of the past nine months, Charlotte wrote: 'A year ago – had a prophet warned me how I should stand in June 1849 – how stripped and bereaved…I should have thought – this can never be endured…'

Charlotte turned to her writing to sustain her through the dark days ahead. Her novel *Shirley*, begun before Branwell's death, was taken up once more. The novel was published in October 1849 and, as winter approached, Charlotte fled Haworth to stay with George Smith and his mother in London. Her fame had provided her with a means of entering London's literary society, but by this time, Charlotte found that her sense of loss and the seclusion of her life at Haworth had left her unfitted to enjoy such society. During her London visit Charlotte was introduced to her literary idol, the novelist W. M. Thackeray, but the experience proved to be more of an ordeal than a pleasure.

Over the next few years there were more visits to London, on one of which she sat for her portrait to the society artist, George Richmond. As Charlotte's true identity gradually became known, her fame brought her a great deal of attention, and in August 1850 she was invited to the summer residence of Sir James and Lady Kay-Shuttleworth above Lake Windermere, where she met the novelist Elizabeth Gaskell. Later in the year, Smith, Elder & Co. gained permission from Newby to reprint *Wuthering Heights* and *Agnes Grey*. Charlotte agreed to edit the work, correcting many of the errors which had appeared in the first edition, and also making changes of her own. She undertook the melancholy task of sorting through her dead sisters' papers to provide a selection of their poetry, and also wrote an emotional biographical notice of the two authors.

Charlotte's last novel, *Villette*, was published in 1853. At this time the atmosphere at the Parsonage was emotionally charged: Charlotte had rejected a marriage proposal from her father's Curate, the

Above: A collection of mourning items and Charlotte Brontë's funeral card.

Reverend Arthur Bell Nicholls, and Patrick was incensed by the mere thought of the poor Irish Curate pursuing his famous daughter. What Charlotte saw as her father's unjust treatment worked in Nicholls' favour, and the couple were eventually married in Haworth Church on 29 June 1854. Though Charlotte had entered the married state with misgivings, she found unexpected happiness with Arthur.

The happiness did not last. Charlotte died on the morning of 31 March 1855, in the early stages of pregnancy, just three weeks before her thirty-ninth birthday. There were to be no direct descendants of the Brontës of Haworth. Patrick Brontë lived on at the Parsonage for a further six years, cared for by his son-in-law, and died there on 7 June 1861, at the age of eighty-four.

In 1857, two years after Charlotte's death, her first novel, *The Professor*, was finally published. In the same year Elizabeth Gaskell's moving tribute to her friend, *The Life of Charlotte Brontë*, also appeared. This biography, along with Charlotte's *Biographical Notice* of her sisters, have become key sources for interpretations of the family, and have ensured that the story of the Brontës' lives continues to exert as much fascination as their fiction.

SCRIBBLEMANIA: THE EARLY WRITINGS

Top: Some of the 'little books' made by the Brontës as children.
Above: The Duke of Zamorna, Byronic hero of the juvenilia, sketched by Branwell.
Left: Branwell's 'Battel Book' from 1827.

From their early childhood, the Brontës created plays and stories, writing them down in the famous handmade 'little books' and developing their characters and themes through adolescence and into adulthood. By the time their novels were accepted for publication in 1847 the Brontës had over twenty years experience of writing and storytelling.

Literary Influences

The Brontës could not afford to purchase a large library. They obtained some newspapers and magazines from friends and the books they did own were read avidly and repeatedly. The Brontës doodled, annotated or wrote their names in many of their books and it has been possible to identify a large number of volumes owned by them. Further evidence of the Brontës' formative reading can be gained from letters and from allusions and quotations found in their own novels. Particular influences were the Bible, Shakespeare, the novels of Walter Scott and the intensely Romantic poetry of Lord Byron. In 1834, Charlotte advised her friend Ellen to read Milton, Shakespeare, Thomson, Goldsmith, Pope, Scott, Byron, Campbell, Wordsworth and Southey. Amongst the family's favourite reading was *Blackwood's Edinburgh Magazine*, which included humour, politics, and travel, providing the basis for both the format and content of much of the Brontës' early writing.

The Early Plays and Little Books

A major catalyst in the creation of the Brontës' imaginary worlds was the arrival of a set of toy soldiers which Mr Brontë purchased for Branwell in June 1826. Both Branwell and Charlotte left accounts

Top Left: Angria and Gondal were very real to the Brontës. This entry for Gondal is sandwiched between real places in the Brontës' copy of Goldsmith's Grammar of General Geography.
Middle: Part of an illustrated manuscript by Branwell, 15 November 1833.
Right: Poetry manuscript by Charlotte, illustrated with a sketch of a woman, c. July 1837.

of how each child selected and named a soldier. For their heroes, Charlotte chose the Duke of Wellington, Branwell Napoleon, Emily one she called Gravey and Anne one called Waiting Boy. The 'Young Men', as the soldiers were known, became 'The Twelves', and their adventures took them to Africa where the Glass Town Confederacy, later to become Angria, was founded. The four children created themselves as the 'Genii' who presided over and protected the Twelves, determining who should live and who should die. Emily and Anne formed their own land, Gondal, which they were able to develop further when Charlotte went away to school in 1831. These early worlds were peopled with a mixture of imaginary and real life public figures, artists, writers and statesmen, and as they developed the characters fought wars, loved and lost, wreaked revenge and suffered.

Patrick was fully aware of his children's writing activities. In a letter to Elizabeth Gaskell, he wrote, 'When mere children, as soon as they could read and write, Charlotte and her brother and sisters used to invent and act little plays of their own … when the argument got warm, and rose to its height, as their mother was then dead, I had sometimes to come in as arbitrator, and settle the dispute according to the best of my judgement.'

The Later Juvenilia

Charlotte and Branwell particularly were ambitious for literary success, and their energetic early collaboration was inspirational, competitive and productive. Branwell wrote to several famous writers of the day, asking advice on how to become a published author. The tone of his surviving letters is naïvely arrogant and he received no reply from *Blackwood's Edinburgh Magazine*, to whom he wrote in 1835 and 1837, or from the poet Wordsworth. Hartley Coleridge responded to Branwell's translations of Horace's Odes with encouragement, but Branwell did not complete his work on this project. In 1837 the twenty year old Charlotte received the now infamous put-down, 'Literature cannot be the business of a woman's life; & it ought not to be', from the Poet Laureate, Robert Southey. However, she treasured his advice that she should write poetry for its own sake, rather than with a view to celebrity, and in later life she believed that his words had made her discipline her writing much more.

As a teacher at Roe Head school from 1835 to 1838, Charlotte suffered great conflict when her teaching duties left her no spare time to retreat into the 'infernal world' of the imagination. What she

Far Left: A fragment written by Charlotte in 1836 when she was a teacher at Roe Head School.
Left: Woman in leopard fur, by Charlotte, October 1839.
Below: Section from Robert Southey's famous letter to the young Charlotte Brontë in which he advised her that 'Literature cannot be the business of a woman's life…'

described as 'scribblemania' was in danger of becoming a passionate obsession, preventing her from fulfilling her everyday tasks. Fragments of prose and poetry written at this time, collectively known as the 'Roe Head Journal', reveal an unhealthy fixation on the imagination and a bitter anger at the prospect of spending the rest of her life as a teacher. In these fragments, Charlotte's characters came to her almost as visions, which were usually interrupted by the mundane routine of school life. On one occasion, in the midst of the creative flow, Charlotte wrote, 'Just then a Dolt came up with a lesson. I thought I should have vomited.'

While a vast number of manuscripts by Charlotte and Branwell have survived, there is little remaining to provide an insight into Emily and Anne's imaginary world of Gondal. Scholars have tried to reconstruct a Gondal chronology from the poems and fragments which exist. Many of Emily and Anne's poems have a

Gondal basis, some of which were reworked, removing the Gondal references, for the 1846 edition of their poems. Even as late as 1845, when Emily was twenty-seven, the sisters were still acting out Gondal scenes.

Much of the Brontës' early work, never intended for publication, is tedious, repetitive and badly spelt; some of it reveals flashes of the brilliance, flair, romance and passion which were to mark their mature writing. It is difficult to determine where the 'juvenilia' ends and the mature work begins. The bulk of the poetry which appeared in the sisters' 1846 collection was written in the 1830s and 1840s as part of the Angria and Gondal sagas, and revised by them for publication. It would be a mistake to see too many parallels between the Brontës' early writings and their novels, but their significance in shaping the mature work cannot be underestimated.

THE POEMS

I n the *Biographical Notice of Ellis and Acton Bell*, published in the 1850 edition of *Wuthering Heights* and *Agnes Grey*, Charlotte recounted how the Brontës came to publish their poems:

'One day, in the autumn of 1845, I accidentally lighted on a MS. volume of verse in my sister Emily's handwriting. Of course, I was not surprised, knowing that she could and did write verse: I looked it over, and something more than surprise seized me, – a deep conviction that these were not common effusions, nor at all like the poetry women generally write. I thought them condensed and terse, vigorous and genuine. To my ear, they had also a peculiar music – wild, melancholy, and elevating.'

The sisters had not been at home together for several years, and obviously Charlotte was unaware how their work had been developing. Emily was extremely angry at the invasion of her privacy and it took some time for Charlotte to persuade her that the poems should be published. Charlotte recalled:

'Averse to personal publicity, we veiled our own names under those of Currer, Ellis, and Acton Bell; the ambiguous choice being dictated by a sort of conscientious scruple at assuming Christian names positively masculine, while we did not like to declare ourselves women, because – without at that time suspecting that our mode of writing and thinking was not what is called 'feminine' – we had a vague impression that authoresses are liable to be looked on with prejudice.'

In the autumn of 1845, Charlotte, Emily and Anne began to select and edit their poems for publication. It is unclear why the sisters chose not to include

Above: Watercolour of wild roses, drawn from nature by Charlotte at the age of fourteen.

Top: Manuscript of one of Emily's poems dated 28 May 1838.
Above: Poetry manuscript by Anne Brontë, 1841-42.
Below: Branwell's The Callousness produced by care, *1842.*

Branwell in their plans, for from 1841 he had seen several of his poems published in the local newspapers. However, just a few months earlier, in July 1845, Branwell had been dismissed from his position as a tutor at Thorp Green and he was in despair at the loss of the woman he loved, Mrs Lydia Robinson. Presumably he was in no fit state to be a part of the scheme. After Branwell's death in 1848 Charlotte told her publisher that her unhappy brother never knew that his sisters had written a line, and that they could not tell him for fear of causing him too much distress. However in a small house like the Parsonage, it would have been difficult to keep letters, proofs and copies of their books a complete secret. Some of Charlotte's mail from the publishers of her novels went astray and it is possible that Branwell may have opened packages by mistake, his sisters' secrecy adding to his grief.

The book was published in a print-run of 1,000 copies by Aylott and Jones of London, costing the sisters around £50.00, a sum funded by legacies from Aunt Branwell. It was difficult for poetry by unknown authors to achieve any success and, despite some favourable reviews, *Poems* sold just two copies. Encouraged by seeing their work in print, the sisters realised that novel writing was more likely to sell.

Charlotte's publishers, Smith, Elder & Co., purchased the unsold copies of *Poems* and re-issued them in 1848. Charlotte acknowledged that her sisters' poetry was superior to her own. Emily is generally recognised as a poet of great power, while Anne's work has a direct simplicity which, like her novels, has been underrated for many years. Branwell's poetry is erratic but some of his shorter, more focused poems approach Emily's in power and clarity of expression. It is in his poetry that we glimpse most strongly what Branwell might have achieved had his life developed along different lines.

Top Left: Signatures of Currer, Ellis and Acton Bell, provided by the Brontës at the request of an early autograph hunter.
Top Right: Charlotte's letter of 16 June 1847 sending a presentation copy of Poems *to the writer J.B. Lockhart, whose work she admired. Copies were also sent to William Wordsworth, Alfred, Lord Tennyson, Thomas De Quincey, Hartley Coleridge and Ebenezer Elliott. She wrote, '…in the space of a year our publisher has disposed but of two copies …'*
Above: The rare first edition of Poems, *published by Aylott and Jones in 1846.*

After Emily's and Anne's deaths, Charlotte included a further selection of poems in the 1850 edition of *Wuthering Heights* and *Agnes Grey*. Keen to protect her sisters' reputations from the literary critics, she edited their works, to the extent of omitting several stanzas from Anne's last, autobiographical poem, 'A dreadful darkness closes in', making her youngest sister seem milder and more accepting of death than she really was.

THE NOVELS

'English Lady' by Charlotte, undated.

Jane Eyre by Charlotte Brontë

Charlotte's most famous novel depicts the emotional and spiritual development of the heroine, which is mirrored by her physical journeyings throughout the book. It describes her search for self-worth, for identity as an individual and for economic independence, in a world which did not expect such ambitions in women.

Jane first appears as an orphaned child, lodged with an aunt who resents her and shamelessly favours her own children. She is sent away to a charity school run by Mr Brocklehurst, where, through the harsh regime, she learns survival and eventually succeeds in becoming a teacher there herself. She advertises for a post as governess, and is appointed to care for Adele, the ward of the sardonic Edward Rochester at Thornfield Hall. Thus far, Charlotte is drawing heavily on her own and her sisters' lives, but it is not an autobiographical novel. The aunt who brought Charlotte up was a benevolent influence. By contrast, her experiences, and those of her sisters, as governesses were far bleaker than that portrayed here. And there was never any Rochester to fall in love with her.

What attracts Rochester to Jane is not her looks (she is small and plain, like her author) but the honesty with which she speaks her mind, and her practical common sense, which enables her to save his life. He proposes marriage, but she discovers at the altar that he already has a wife, Bertha, a lunatic who is kept in the attic at Thornfield. Jane refuses to become Rochester's mistress, and flees from him. Destitute, she is taken in by the Rivers family, who, coincidentally, turn out to be cousins, and reveal that

she is heiress to sufficient funds to give her financial security for life. The Revd. St. John Rivers, who is planning to go to India as a missionary, asks her to marry him and follow him in his calling. Jane is on the point of acceptance, when she hears a supernatural cry from Rochester. She returns to Thornfield to find that the house has been burned down by Bertha, and that Rochester himself has been maimed and blinded in an unsuccessful attempt to save his wife. Now, Jane can marry him, not just because he is widowed but because his physical dependence gives her the equality to which she aspires.

Elements of the uncanny, the fairy tale and the supernatural abound in *Jane Eyre*. Storms and fires reflect the psychological turmoil of the protagonists, while hauntings and transformations give a sense of dream or nightmare.

The world through which Jane moves has a strong moral dimension (unlike *Wuthering Heights*) which initially oppresses her, but which she confronts and finally comes to terms with. Brocklehurst and St. John Rivers are pillars of the church, but their stony formalism precludes real emotional warmth. Jane has to seek her own salvation, but she does so in traditional Christian terms; by sacrificing her prospective life with Rochester, she ultimately saves it, herself and him.

Wuthering Heights by Emily Brontë

The structure of *Wuthering Heights* is complex: the narrator is Lockwood, Heathcliff's shadowy tenant at Thrushcross Grange. He learns the history of the Earnshaws and the Lintons from Ellen ('Nellie') Dean, who has been a servant at both Wuthering Heights and Thrushcross Grange, and whose account fills most of the book. Within that story, the characters come to life and speak with their own individual voices.

Ellen's account begins with the father of Catherine and Hindley Earnshaw returning home with an orphan child, whom he names Heathcliff and who becomes his favourite. Heathcliff and Catherine develop a passionate love, while mutual hatred grows between Heathcliff and Hindley. After Mr Earnshaw's death, Hindley humiliates Heathcliff, who endures everything on account of his love, until he overhears Catherine tell Ellen that it would degrade her to marry him. Catherine has met Edgar and Isabella, the children of the Linton family at Thrushcross Grange, and Edgar has proposed to her. She accepts, and Heathcliff vanishes.

Three years later, Heathcliff returns as abruptly as he left. The petulant adolescent has changed into a master schemer whose twin passions, love and desire for revenge, are thinly masked by wealth and an air of gentility. He lodges with Hindley, who is now widowed with a young son, Hareton. He encourages Hindley's drunkenness and gambling, and wins from him the deeds to Wuthering Heights. He renews his association with Catherine, to the dismay of her effete husband Edgar, but then elopes with Isabella, whom

Left: Drawing of a fir tree by Emily, c. 1842.

he maltreats. Catherine becomes pregnant, and a sudden irruption by Heathcliff induces her labour: she dies giving birth to Cathy. Isabella escapes to London, where she has a son, giving him her maiden name of Linton.

Step by step, Heathcliff takes control of the younger generation. After Hindley's death, he brutalises Hareton in revenge for his own treatment. Isabella, too, dies, and he seizes their son, Linton, whom Edgar had sought to care for. Finally, he decoys Cathy to Wuthering Heights where he forces her to marry Linton. In this way, he gains control of both houses, and obliterates both family names. Edgar and Linton die in turn. Cathy develops an affection for Hareton, and the possibility emerges of eventual happiness and redemption. The fulfilment of Heathcliff's plan should have been the destruction of them both, but his vindictiveness has worn him out, and his only desire is to be reunited with Catherine beyond the grave. He wastes away, and the novel ends with village gossip of their ghosts being seen together on the moors.

Two crucial features of the book are its Gothic qualities, and the lack of moral comment from its author. The presence of ghosts and visions, the prevalence of storms and darkness (echoing the characters' turbulent emotions) and – at the core – Heathcliff's diabolical nature, combine with the melodramatic plot to create a violent nightmare into which the reader is sucked. The wild, stormy landscape, and Wuthering Heights itself, with its air of faded grandeur and atmosphere of spiritual gloom owe much to the Gothic novels of the late eighteenth century. What is exceptional for the period is the absence of explicit condemnation by Emily of Heathcliff's conduct, or any suggestion that evil might bring its own punishment. The novel is morally ambiguous, the author leaving us to draw our own conclusions. This led to criticism by many early readers, but is an important aspect of its contemporary appeal.

Agnes Grey by Anne Brontë

Agnes Grey is the daughter of a clergyman whose financial imprudence leads to the family's ruin. The women take charge, but Agnes fears that, being the

Above: Horton Lodge, the home of the Murray family, by E. M. Wimperis, 1872.

baby of the family, she will be prevented from making any real contribution, and she insists on seeking work as a governess.

She first goes to the Bloomfield family, and takes charge of what seem like infant fiends. The familiar fate of the governess, being neither servant nor family member, is well analysed, and Agnes finds herself involved with three generations of the family, eventually finding favour with none of them. Her efforts to combat the barbarity of the children and the undue partiality of the parents are doomed, and she is dismissed.

In her second position with the Murrays, where her pupils are older, she is more successful, but this is a family for whom social values are more important than moral ones, and she fears the gradual degeneration of the values instilled into her at home. The saving figures in her life are poor people she visits, and the clergyman Edward Weston, for whom she feels first respect, then love. Gradually she sees her eldest pupil committing herself to a marriage for purely mercenary and social reasons, and she seizes the chance, when her father dies, to set up with her mother a school in a seaside town based on Scarborough. It is on the sands of that town that she is reunited with Mr Weston and her beloved dog Snap.

Anne's first novel resembles in its calm naturalism nothing so much as one of the later Austen novels, with the vital difference that her heroine is a working woman. It deserves, far more than *Jane Eyre*, the description 'governess novel', because Agnes's experience is far more typical, and the predicament of the occupation is analysed much more closely. Though the novel never raises its voice it has some sharp comic scenes, some devastating analyses of character (for example that of the worldly, pushy clergyman Mr Hatfield) and a deft hand with pathos, particularly the pathos of emotional deprivation.

THE NOVELS

The Tenant of Wildfell Hall by Anne Brontë

The tenant of the title is Helen Huntingdon, who, under the name Mrs Graham, arrives at the decaying Elizabethan mansion and causes gossip and rumour to spread in the neighbourhood. She arouses the interest of Gilbert Markham, a local farmer, and though she tries to repel his growing love for her, his closeness to her young son eventually makes her treat him in a more friendly fashion. The relationship however is hindered by the opposition and ridicule of his family, and by the figure of Frederick Lawrence, who seems to have an interest in or influence over the mysterious tenant which arouses Gilbert's antagonism. After the pair fight, 'Mrs Graham' thrusts into Gilbert's hands a diary which tells the story of her disastrous marriage.

A serious and pious young girl, she has become fascinated by a young man of bad reputation, Arthur Huntingdon, a Byronic figure of great fascination but also of hardly-concealed moral failings. She marries him, fatally confident that her love will reform him. For a time all goes well, but gradually he resumes his drinking and womanising, and Helen becomes increasingly unhappy. A son is born, but her husband's debaucheries become more frequent and more organised. When he begins to corrupt his son into his own 'manly' habits she decides to flee, and after an aborted attempt, sadistically thwarted by her husband, she finally achieves her aim, fleeing to Wildfell Hall, in the vicinity of her brother, who is Frederick Lawrence.

When Arthur is on his death-bed, Helen returns to him and watches helplessly as he dies unrepentant. After some delays and misunderstandings she marries Gilbert Markham.

The novel was so unsparing in its depiction of drunkenness and debauchery that Charlotte tried to prevent any reprinting of it after her sister's death. Anne's aim, however, was entirely to warn by depicting vice as it really is, unattractive and soul-destroying. Many modern critics have seen parallels in the novel to *Wuthering Heights*, signalled by the W.H. house name and plethora of characters whose names begin with H, but more importantly in the similar themes covered: drunkenness, corruption of children, mistreatment of women and so on. They have believed Anne wished to set these things in a proper moral context, something conspicuously lacking in her sister's novel. However that may be, the novel has certainly increased in reputation in our own time. Many find the moralising too insistent, but it is firmly grounded in situation and characters, and the stern tone is mitigated by the discussions of the doctrine of universal redemption.

Above:'What you please', a sketch by Anne, 1840.

Shirley by Charlotte Brontë

As many critics have noted, *Shirley* has a number of different plot strands which are loosely drawn together and the novel can be read as a romantic tale, as sociological comment on the question of womens' lives or as a history of the Luddite riots in the cloth making district of Yorkshire.

Above: Hollow's Mill by E. M. Wimperis, 1872.

The novel is set in 1811-12 in the period of Luddite riots with Robert Moore, tenant of Hollow's-mill, encountering trouble when he tries to bring in new equipment.

Moore lives at Hollow's cottage with his sister Hortense, who teaches Caroline Helstone, niece of the rector of Briarfield. One evening after Caroline has been dining with Moore and his sister, she realises that she is in love with Moore, and believes him to feel the same about her. Caroline's tedious and oppressed life at the Rectory is evoked with descriptions of visits by Mrs Sykes and her daughters and of visits by the three local curates.

Mr Helstone and Moore quarrel and Caroline's uncle forbids her from having anything further to do with the Moores. Caroline herself has felt uncertain due to Moore's changeability. She determines to try to prepare herself for life without marriage, visiting two elderly spinsters, Miss Mann and Miss Ainley. Under the influence of Miss Ainley, Caroline decides that she must do more to help the poor of the area.

Mr Helstone introduces Caroline to Shirley Keeldar, who has just come into her inheritance and is living nearby at Fieldhead. There, she also meets Mrs Pryor, Shirley's former governess and now companion. Caroline becomes good friends with the fiercely independent Shirley and forms a strong attachment to the gentle Mrs Pryor.

Caroline still hopes to meet Moore on her frequent walks and one evening sees him talking to Shirley. Caroline later confesses to her maid that she thinks that Moore will marry Shirley. Moore is reconciled with Mr Helstone; soon after this Hollow's-mill is attacked. Moore is wounded and Shirley has to prevent Caroline from rushing to him.

Shirley's relatives, the Sympson family, arrive to stay at Fieldhead. While visiting Hortense, Caroline meets Louis Moore, Robert's brother, who is tutor to Henry Sympson, Shirley's young cousin. Hortense suggests that Robert Moore is favoured by Shirley. Caroline falls into a grave illness and Mrs Pryor is sent by Shirley to nurse her. Mrs Pryor reveals that she is Caroline's mother, her real name is Agnes Helstone. Caroline, given a reason to live, recovers.

A number of incidents occur in which Louis Moore shows tender feelings towards Shirley, his former pupil. The strength of Louis Moore's feelings are made clear to the reader as he broods over her desk in her absence. Shirley has had several proposals of marriage which she has rejected despite pressure from the Sympsons and on a journey with Mr Yorke, Robert Moore confesses that he proposed to Shirley some time ago and was rejected. On the same journey Moore is shot at and wounded and is taken to Mr Yorke's house to recover. Yorke's young son arranges for Caroline to see Moore, which helps his recovery.

Louis and Shirley declare their love. Moore proposes to Caroline and she accepts. Moore states that Caroline has changed his views and that in future he will take on more workers and that she shall set up a Sunday School. The novel ends with a double wedding.

THE NOVELS

Villette by Charlotte Brontë

Villette – 'little town' – is a rather condescending description of Brussels, the city where Lucy Snowe and her creator, Charlotte Brontë, worked as schoolteachers and had deep emotional experiences. Charlotte's last completed novel is her most autobiographical and most complex. Less happens, in terms of external events, but the internal lives of its characters are more intense than in any Brontë work. Some readers have found the psychological switchbacks unsatisfactory, but – for many – the knowledge that most individuals are a mass of contradictions make *Villette* a highly realistic novel.

The story, in essence, is simple. Lucy Snowe, an orphan, stays as a child with Mrs Bretton her godmother, Graham the son of the house, and Polly, who has been left in Mrs Bretton's care by her father who is grieving over the death of a frivolous wife – Ginevra. Lucy first finds work as a lady's companion, and then travels to Villette to seek employment.

Lucy takes a post at a girls' school, where one of the students is Ginevra Fanshawe, the niece (and spiritual heir) of Polly's mother. At the Pensionnat, she studies under and teaches alongside M Paul Emanuel, a waspish martinet with a heart of gold

Above: Illustration to Villette *by Edmund Dulac.*

whom women love and fear, while he himself remains indifferent to them.

Lucy recognises the school doctor, John Bretton, to be Graham, her childhood friend, and has to repress her feelings of attraction as she sees his infatuation with the flirtatious Ginevra. Meanwhile, unnoticed by Lucy (but obvious to the reader), M Emanuel is falling in love with her, rather against his will and much against the wishes of other acquaintances whose interest lies in keeping him heart-whole. He angrily observes Lucy's affection for Bretton, but this is extinguished by the reappearance of Polly, whom the doctor rescues from a fire and recognises as his soul-mate.

Paul announces that he must go to the West Indies for three years to take care of the family investment there. As a final act of generosity, he presents Lucy with a school of her own. As the novel ends, he is about to return to Europe. Charlotte leaves us with a storm at sea and uncertainty whether M Paul survives it.

Villette is a reworking of material from Charlotte's first novel, *The Professor* (then still unpublished), and depicts, thinly-disguised, her passion for M Heger, her

Above: The Pensionnat by E.M.Wimperis, 1872.

Brussels schoolmaster, and her attraction to George Smith, her young publisher. Many elements echo *Jane Eyre*: both have orphans as heroines, plain women who have to find their way through an alien world. Lucy Snowe (in drafts for the book, Charlotte alternated between Snow[e] and Frost, showing the importance of the name as representing coldness) is an outsider; in appearance a self-composed observer, in reality a mass of emotions which she can only control by suppression. Sometimes she confides in the reader; often, even we must guess at what is in her mind. By contrast, M Emanuel is fiery and choleric, but internally is cool until Lucy's coldness warms him.

The novel retains many gothic elements: far-fetched coincidences, ghosts and dream-like sequences, which contend with its prevailing realism. Its predominantly sombre mood is intensified rather than lightened, by moments of bleak humour. These contradictions, which made it unsatisfactory for many Victorian readers, are precisely what make it so appealing to many twentieth century ones.

The Professor by Charlotte Brontë

The central character of Charlotte's first novel, William Crimsworth, is an orphan, educated by a cold, indifferent family of maternal relatives. Freeing himself from them, William goes to work in the industrial North for his brother Edward, but finds him a sadistic tyrant. Influenced by his friend Yorke Hunsden, he decides to try his fortunes on the Continent.

With the aid of an introduction from Hunsden he finds work as a teacher in a local boys' school run by M Pelet, with additional work at a neighbouring establishment for girls whose head is the exotically-named Zoraide Reuter. He soon finds himself embroiled in a triangle which is partly sexual, partly a manoeuvring for power. Crimsworth's instincts are generally towards observation and disengagement rather than involvement, and he coolly takes steps to extricate himself. He is helped by his growing interest

in a pupil-teacher at Mme Reuter's school, Frances Henri, of Anglo-Swiss parentage. Gradually a love relationship develops, as teacher-pupil relationships often do in Charlotte's novels, in this case seen from the point of view of the male.

Intervention by Zoraide Reuter threatens the burgeoning love of William and Frances, but this forces him to engage himself emotionally, bring his love out in the open, and act decisively. The pair marry, but Frances insists on maintaining her independence by running a school. They return to England, and the novel ends with calm domestic happiness, marred only by worries about the unduly tender-hearted nature of their son, whom William fears to be unfit for the hardness of the world.

The novel is low-key and, like *Agnes Grey*, rather out-of-step with the generality of Brontë novels. The traditional complaint that Crimsworth is a man as imagined by a woman sounds rather dated now, and he can be seen as an over-cool, repressed, but morally sophisticated product of his upbringing. The theme of antagonistic brothers comes from the juvenile writings and finds its way into many Brontë novels. The apparently unsensational story-line and the even tenor of its narration have prevented the novel gaining wide popularity, though there are signs that this estimation is changing.

Above: Pensionnat Heger viewed from the Rue d'Isabelle.

THE BRONTË SOCIETY & THE BRONTË PARSONAGE MUSEUM

The Brontë Society, which administers the Brontë Parsonage Museum, was founded by a small group of enthusiasts in 1893. Many literary societies founded in this period did not survive, but the dedication of its early members held the Brontë Society together, and its reputation spread far beyond the West Riding of Yorkshire where it had originated. Today the Brontë Society is one of the most important literary societies in the world.

One of the Society's main objectives was to establish a Museum to contain drawings, manuscripts,

paintings, and other personal relics of the Brontë family, editions of their works, writings on these works and on the family, and photographs of places with which they were associated.

A small museum was established in 1895, in a room above Haworth's Yorkshire Penny Bank (now the Tourist Information Centre), but from its foundation the Brontë Society had hoped to acquire Haworth Parsonage, which in the years after Patrick Brontë's death served as home to four further incumbents. By 1927 the Brontë Society's Collection had outgrown the crowded one-room museum, and at this point, when the Society's cash assets stood at less than fifty pounds, the Church Trustees announced they were prepared to sell the Parsonage for a sum of three thousand pounds.

Sir James Roberts, who was to describe himself as 'one of the fast narrowing circle of Haworth veterans who remember the Parsonage family', offered not only to buy the Parsonage, but to contribute £500 towards the cost of establishing it as a Museum and Library. On 4 August 1928 a crowd of thousands arrived in Haworth to witness Sir James present the title deeds to the Society.

Over the years the Brontë Society has sought to restore the Parsonage to its appearance in the Brontës' time. Although the household goods had been scattered far and wide after Patrick Brontë's death, many items were eventually returned. Today the Society continues to care for the family's former home, and collects, preserves and exhibits material relating to the Brontës' lives and works, making them known to a wider audience.

Left: The first Brontë Museum above Haworth's Yorkshire Penny Bank.
Below: In 1928 thousands turned out to see the opening of the Brontë Parsonage Museum.